TURN IT TO GOLD

Turn It to Gold

D. James Kennedy

VINE
BOOKS
Servant Publications
Ann Arbor, Michigan

Vine Books is an imprint of Servant Publications especially
designed to serve Evangelical Christians.

Published by Servant Publications
P.O. Box 8617
Ann Arbor, Michigan 48107

Cover design by Michael Andaloro
Cover photo Larime Photographic
    93 94 95   10 9 8 7 6 5

Printed in the United States of America
ISBN 0-89283-633-4

Library of Congress Cataloging-in-Publication Data

Kennedy, D. James (Dennis James), 1930-
    Turn it to gold / D. James Kennedy
        p.   cm.
ISBN 0-89283-633-4
    1. Consolation. 2. Suffering—Religious aspects—
Christianity.   I. Title.
BV4905.2.K46 1991
248.8'6—dc20   91-10313

Contents

ONE

The Alchemy of God

And we know that all things work together for good to them that love God, to them who are the called according to his purpose. **Romans 8:28**

ALCHEMY WAS THE PRECURSOR of chemistry, in somewhat the same way that astrology was the forerunner of astronomy. The great quest of the alchemists was to transform something common into something precious: to change lead into gold.

They failed in their quest. However, God is the great cosmic alchemist who *never* fails. In this book, we'll look at the incredible ways God changes the "lead" of our lives into gold.

Our world is full of the inexplicable, the inscrutable, the unfathomable, the impassable, and the insurmountable. We cannot take three steps in any direction without running into a solid wall of mysteries, riddles, paradoxes, and profundities. We constantly confront problems we cannot solve, labyrinths we cannot find our way out of, hieroglyphics we cannot decipher, sphinxes that simply will not speak. Life is full of puzzles!

BAD THINGS *DO* HAPPEN

When we face the avalanche of trials and troubles that come upon us, we cry out, "*Why*, God? Why *me*? Why *now*?" God takes all those questions, gathers them up in his arms, and writes over them the majestic words of Romans 8:28: "*All things work together for good to them that love God.*"

This is one of the greatest texts in all of Scripture. No other verse covers so much territory or conveys so much comfort and hope.

Unfortunately, for many people no other text seems more difficult to believe. In light of all the problems we know in this life, some would say that it cannot possibly be true. Loved ones have been lost. Homes have been shattered. Children have been taken away. Spouses are even now in the hospital. "How," they ask, "can these awful realities work together for good? How I wish it could be true!"

Do you believe that God is working all things together for good in your life? That every happening in your life must pay interest to the eternal well-being of your soul?

What a glorious truth! Think how much anxiety we would be spared if we could truly come to believe this wonderful truth.

Well, the Lord *wants* us to be able to believe it. He wants us to be able to say, with the apostle Paul, "I *know* that all things work together for good to them that love God!"

Let's look more carefully at this verse, to see what it has to say to us.

IS EVERYTHING GOOD?

First, let's note what Romans 8:28 does *not* say. It does not say that *everything* is good. Indeed, many things in this world are anything but good. Diseases, accidents, wars, hurricanes, earthquakes—these are certainly not good.

Yet God makes it clear that whatever event comes upon us, no matter how grim or ghastly in itself, as soon as it touches our lives, the hand of God will reach down and take it captive. And God will not let go until it yields up its treasure to our soul. That is the promise of the Almighty.

GOOD FOR WHOM?

Paul does not say that all things will work together for good for *everyone*. There is a maxim, part of the wisdom of this world, which says that everything works out for the best for everyone. I would be unfaithful to the Word of God if I left you with that impression from this verse. It does not say that.

Indeed, everything does *not* work out for the best for most people. Jesus made it very clear: "There are few who find the way to life and many who enter into destruction (see Matthew 7:13-14). People who live ungodly lives and do not trust in Christ sooner or later have their lives filled with illness, decay, dissolution, and death. They plunge into that pit from which no man returns. That is not working out anything for good.

No, our text says that it is *to those who love God, to those who are called according to his purpose,* to those whom he has chosen and called and justified, that he works everything together for good. This grace of God is for his own people, those who have repented of their sins and cast themselves upon his mercy.

Otherwise, instead of all things working together for good, we could expect just the opposite to occur. If we do not let them lead to recognition of God's mercy and to repentance of our sin, all the blessings that God has seen fit to pour out upon our heads will ultimately work to our destruction and condemnation.

There are two antithetical principles at work in this world. If we have repented and trusted in Jesus Christ, then even evil will be transformed into good. If we live in rebellion and unbelief, then even what is good will finally work for evil. "Go to now, ye rich men, weep and howl for your miseries that shall come upon you. Your riches are corrupted, and your garments are moth-eaten. Your gold and silver is cankered . . ." (James 5:1-3).

Yes, even the good things that the unbeliever receives in this world will stand as an accusing witness against him at the judgment, because they have not led to repentance and to faith in the one who is the source of those blessings.

WORKED TOGETHER BY GOD

Furthermore, Paul does not say that things work to-gether for good *naturally all by themselves.* We may not see this clearly in the English translation. What Paul actually said in the Greek text is this: "For we know that unto those who love God, *God* works all things together for good."

It is God who is supernaturally making all things work together for our good. The almighty alchemist takes whatever ingredients come into our lives and combines them to produce a good result. God turns them to gold.

ALL THINGS?

Part of the wonder is that God does this with *everything* that comes our way. Now, if Paul had simply said that "a *few* things work together for our good," or "*some* things," or even "*many* things," we would not so much as raise an eyebrow. But what he said was "*all things*."

And we know this verse was not penned by a fair-weather soldier, an ivory-tower theologian who had never been in the trenches. Paul was a weather-beaten warrior for Christ. He could catalog enormous difficulties in his life: hunger, thirst, loneliness, sickness, imprisonment, robberies, stonings, scourgings, shipwrecks, assassination attempts, trial and condemnation at the hand of the evil emperor Nero himself.

No, Paul knew the harsh realities of life and had the scars to prove it. And it was in the midst of earning those scars that he could assure us that God works all things together for good. "The things which happened unto me," he once said, "have fallen out rather unto the furtherance of the gospel" (Philippians 1:12).

SPIRITUAL SYNERGY

"All things," said Paul, "work *together*." The Greek word here is *sunergeo*, from which we get the English word "synergy." Synergy is when two or more things interact to produce a result greater than the mere sum of their parts.

All things work *together*, not separately. Suppose a physician prescribes some medicine for us. We take the prescription to the pharmacist. He gathers the various chemicals from his shelves and mixes them together with mortar and pestle.

Often among such ingredients may be found substances which, by themselves, would be harmful to our health. For example, arsenic is found in many medicines. Were we to take it by itself, this poison would kill us.

Yet when a potentially dangerous ingredient is mixed together with others, that same chemical may produce something beneficial to our health. So it is with God's action in our lives.

Thus we learn that we cannot look at any particular, single event and say, "How is *this* working for my good?" We may not ever know. It is not singular events, not individual ingredients, but *all things working together* that God uses to advance our spiritual well-being.

"I DON'T KNOW HOW"

Charles Spurgeon, the famous English preacher, tells of a man who was arrested during the reign of Queen Mary for preaching the gospel. The prisoner was swiftly condemned to be burned at the stake. When he heard the sentence he said, "Never mind; all things work together for good."

People asked, "But how is this going to work for your good?" He replied, "I do not know *how*. But I know that it *will*."

On the way to London the guards treated him so roughly that they cast him down and broke his leg. They mocked him, saying, "Tell us, how is this going to work for your good?" Again the prisoner said calmly, "I do not know. But I know that God will use it to bring good."

The man's leg was splinted so that he could continue the trip. Because of the accident, the party arrived in London one day later than planned—and, as it happened, one day after Queen Mary had died. Elizabeth was now on the throne. The man was pardoned.

FOR WHAT GOOD?

God works all things together for good, but not always for "good" in the sense that those in the world would conceive of it. They would label as good only that which advanced their prosperity or gratified their earthly desires.

But God is talking about our *spiritual* good, our growth in grace, our being conformed to the image of Jesus Christ. Sometimes things may work toward the very opposite of our apparent earthly good. God often blesses us in this world and turns our adversities to our advantage in the here and now. But ultimately he is pursuing our spiritual advancement. I do not believe there is a single person who knows the Lord Jesus Christ who could not testify to some adversity that has greatly advanced his or her spiritual progress. It is our *eternal* well-being that God most desires.

A THREE-ACT PLAY

A man recommended a play to his friend. "It's marvelous," he said. "You'll love it. It's so uplifting and exhilarating. You'll be greatly encouraged."

He was astonished when his friend later reported, "I *hated* that play! I thought it was terrible. Why, the child was kidnapped, the father lost his job, and the mother ended up in the hospital. It was so depressing! How could you have thought a play like that was good?"

The first man said, "But that's not the way it wound up. Didn't you stay to the end?"

"No," his friend replied. "I was so depressed, I left after the second act!"

There is a final act to life. We pass through a curtain that leads to the final act of the drama of God's redemption. If we did not know that, we could not believe that all things will ultimately work together for our good. Sometimes the good is withheld until the life to come, when God will right all wrongs. Then, perfectly and completely and finally, God will make all things work together for good *for those who love him.*

THE GREAT DIVIDE

Let me emphasize again that we find here a truth that appears frequently in Scripture. God divides mankind into two great camps: those who love him and those who do not.

This is truly humanity's great divide. Different Christians may approach some doctrines differently, but we are all called to love God with all our heart and soul and mind and strength. If we have been redeemed by Christ, if we have been forgiven by him and adopted into his family, if we have been given the free gift of eternal life through faith in him, the inevitable result is that we love Jesus Christ.

Many people delude themselves into thinking that they love God. They create in their own minds a god after their own likeness, and then profess their love for *that* god. But the God of the Scriptures, the God and Father of our Lord Jesus Christ, the God of Abraham, Isaac, and Jacob—*this* God they shrink from. Why? Because the burden of their guilt is upon them, and they cannot look up at a holy and righteous God.

Only when we have trusted in Christ, when we have repented of our sins, when we have been reconciled to the Father through Jesus Christ, is our guilt taken away so that we can lift up our eyes and say, "Father, I love you!"

DIFFERENT LENSES

Do you love God in that way? Reconciliation to God makes a major difference in the way we respond to adversity. Love helps us view difficulties through different lenses.

"I myself perceived also that one event happeneth to them all" (Ecclesiastes 2:14). Some things are common to all men and women: sorrow, grief, loss, suffering, temptation, death.

Yet these common experiences do not yield the same results. God makes the sun to shine upon the good and the evil, and sends the rain on the just and the unjust alike, but with differing results. The same sun that bakes bricks also melts butter. Adversity leads some people to become embittered and hardened, hateful toward God and man. Others are sweetened and softened.

Jesus told a parable about two houses. The rains descended, and the winds blew, and the floods came and beat upon the two houses. All of the same elements afflicted both. Yet one stood secure, while the other fell—and, said Jesus, "great was the fall of it" (see Matthew 7:24-27).

So it is with those who love God. They yield far different fruit when the adversities of life come upon them. Those who love God have been called according to the eternal purpose of the one who, before the foundation of the world, determined to reach down into the very mire of sin and to lift up a multitude of souls that no man can number . . . to cleanse them from the vileness of their iniquity . . . to wash them and make them whiter than snow . . . to refashion them into the image of his Son . . . to take them to be with him forever in paradise. What a glorious truth! For them that love him, God works all things together for good!

THE ALCHEMY OF GOD

I urge you to take hold of this truth. Grasp it firmly with the hand of faith. Lean upon it. Launch out upon it into the stormy seas, and let God take away the worries, the fears, the anxieties for the future.

Lead into gold. Trials into triumphs. This is the alchemy of God!

Let's look further into this marvelous passage of Scripture to see what it shows us about the transcendent plan and purpose of God in our lives.

TWO

God's Sovereign Plan

If God is for us, who can be against us? He who did not spare his own Son, but gave him up for us—how will he also, along with him, graciously give us all things.

Romans 8:31-32

GOD IS AT WORK to redeem us and forgive us and one day take us to be with him forever in paradise. But God's love will not settle for that alone. He is also actively working to transform all things, by the incredible alchemy of his grace, into good. This is a truth so profound that I am sure we will never plumb its depths.

But how desperately we need this truth! In the midst of a universe that seems quite inhospitable, we live on a tiny planet made up of molten rock with a hard crust relatively less thick than the skin of an apple. Above us are cosmic rays that would fry us to a crisp were they not filtered through a God-ordained layer of atmosphere. Broiled from below or fried from above—we live on a very precarious planet indeed!

As if that were not enough, we are part of a civilization where people more often act like wolves and tigers than human beings. Every day we hear reports of murders, rapes, muggings, and robberies.

Truly in many ways we live in an inhospitable world. How desperately we need to know that there is a Father who cares—and, more than that, a Father who is for us and is working all things together for our good.

A MARVELOUS PLAN

How can this be? Romans 8:28 begins with an important conjunction, "*And* we know that all things work together for the good..." The word "*and*" tells us that what follows it is intimately related to what has gone before. Just prior to this verse, Paul has told us that God has indwelt us by his Holy Spirit, who is working mightily within us. It is by that indwelling Spirit that God is moving in our lives to bring to pass his marvelous plan.

God has a wonderful plan for this world! It is a plan whose architectural drawings were made in eternity. It encompasses the most minute detail. When time has run its course, when the final curtain has been lowered, we will discover that God's plan has been worked out to its tiniest detail—that his will has, indeed, been done.

Our God is perfect in all his attributes. Perfect in his power. Perfect in his holiness and justice. Perfect in his love and mercy. Perfect in his knowledge and wisdom. Therefore his plan must also be perfect!

That is an amazing and comforting idea. It often seems as if the world is careening along unattended, like a chariot whose driver has fallen off. The horses are running wild, the reins are flying in the wind. The runaway chariot is threatening to plunge over the precipice at any moment.

Yet the Scriptures teach us that God, the sovereign Lord of history, has his hands firmly upon the reigns, and that his perfect plan *is* coming to pass.

This is not to deny that the world is filled with many evil things. It is not to shut our eyes to those realities, but to open our eyes to the realization that God sovereignly overwhelms all these things to bring about his will.

Even though Lucifer loosed chaos in the very midst of heaven, God who created Lucifer knew precisely what this rebellious angel would do. He knew of the sin that would be introduced into the peaceful calm of paradise. God knew of the malignant envy and vain ambition that would lead Lucifer to rebel. God even knew that sin would necessarily require his own perfect judgment: sickness, death, disillusionment, decay. Yet God permitted all these things. Why? *So that he might overcome them with good!*

NO ASSISTANCE NEEDED

God has a perfect plan—a plan that requires no human assistance.

Near Madrid, Spain, stands one of the greatest palaces ever built by man. It is called the Escorial. For centuries the kings and queens of Spain have been buried there. It incorporates the vast church of San Lorenzo.

When this magnificent building was under construction, the architect designed a vast arch, larger than any ever built before. Upon that arch would rest the entire weight of the church's massive roof. The king was worried that the tremendous weight of the roof would be more than the arch could bear. So he ordered the architect to build a column from the floor all the way to the center of the arch, to prop it up. The architect protested vehemently that it was not needed. But the king insisted and, over the lamentations of the architect, the column was built. The king worshiped contentedly, having seen to it himself that the ceiling would not fall.

Years went by. The king finally died. Only then did the architect reveal that he had left a quarter-inch space between the top of the column and the arch it was supposedly supporting. In the hundreds of years that have since passed, that arch has not sagged so much as a quarter of an inch. If you were to visit the Escorial today, you could watch a tour guide pass a board between the column and the arch, vindicating the design of that long-ago architect.

So it is with the plan of God, that over-arching plan that encompasses all of life, all of reality. It needs no human support to prop it up. God himself is the designer and the sustainer, and this very same God is working out his purposes in our lives.

GOD'S MYSTERIOUS WAYS

Have you ever heard the familiar expression, "God works in mysterious ways his wonders to perform?" It comes from an old hymn written by a man named William Cowper.

At the time, Cowper was not a Christian. His life was in shambles and he was filled with despair, so much so that he decided to take his life by swallowing poison.

Cowper did not die, but became terribly ill. He bought a gun and tried to shoot himself. But the gun did not go off. So he threw it away, got a rope, and tried to hang himself. The rope broke. In utter desperation, Cowper hired a carriage in London and instructed the driver to take him to the Thames River. He planned to jump in and drown himself. But the driver could not find the Thames! The fog had settled in so thickly that even a London cabbie got lost!

Finally Cowper went back to his room. His eyes fell upon a Bible, which he opened and began to read. The book told of a heavenly Father who loved even William Cowper. Astonished by the events that had just taken place, he read of the sovereign providence of God working all things together for good according to his own divine plan and purpose. Cowper embraced Jesus Christ as his Lord and Savior and in gratitude wrote these wonderful words:

God moves in a mysterious way
　　His wonders to perform;
He plants his footsteps in the sea
　　And rides upon the storm.

You fearful saints, fresh courage take;
　　The clouds you so much dread
Are big with mercy, and shall break
　　in blessings on your head.

Judge not the Lord by feeble sense
　　But trust him for his grace;
Behind a frowning providence
　　He hides a smiling face.

His purposes will ripen fast,
  Unfolding every hour;
The bud may have a bitter taste,
  But sweet will be the flower.

Blind unbelief is sure to err,
  And scan his work in vain;
God is his own interpreter,
  And he will make it plain.

NO CONTRADICTIONS

"We know," Paul says, "that God is working all things together for our good." Did you ever stop to think that it would be a marvelous thing if God did that even without telling us about it? But how much more wonderful that he *does* tell us! We can *know* for certain that he has a perfect plan for us, and that within the context of that plan he is working all things together for our good.

Still, the sad fact is that many people forget this. Don't we all lose sight of this truth at times? I wish the words could be seared into the consciousness of each and every one of us: *God is working all things together for our good!*

The universe, in one sense, is like a vast machine that is constantly in motion. The sun, the moon, the planets, even the farthest stars, continually fulfill their God-ordained functions. The oceans, rivers, and trees perform the work that God gives them to do. There is no silent nook in the deepest forest glade where there is not work going on—

work ordained by God to accomplish his plan.

We might, as we look around, think that the world works in complete contradiction, that everything works against everything else. And yet Romans 8:28 tells us that everything works *together* for our good.

There is no contradiction in the plan of God. Even the raven wing of war is not in opposition to the dove of peace. The fiercest storm does not contradict the most peaceful calm. The heat and the cold, the rain and the sun, all work together for good. The light and darkness of our lives work together in the great plan that God has ordained.

EVEN SIN!

What about sin? Even here, we see that the sins of men can be used by God to produce good.

Remember Naomi's son, who married Ruth the Moabite woman? (see Ruth 1:4). You may not have realized that this was serious sin. God had forbidden the Israelites to marry those from other nations. Yet God overcame this sin and made Ruth one of the ancestors of David, and thus of the Messiah.

Or remember Simon. At the most critical juncture, he denied Christ three times. But God used that denial, and the subsequent tears of remorse, to fuse the sands of Simon's character into Peter, the rock.

If God could not work with sinful men and women, he could not work in this world at all, because there are no other men and women available! God took the worst sin ever committed, the crucifixion of the spotless son of God, and made it the source of the greatest blessings humankind has ever known.

Even *our* own sin can work for good. This is hard for us to accept. As we look into the mirror of our lives, we may be pleased with the reflection that greets our eyes. But when we fall prey to temptation and sin stains our countenance, we look again with horror and cannot stand the ugly sight. Then suddenly, in the background, we see the cross of Calvary where Jesus died to save us. There, against the reflection of our own iniquity, we see all the more clearly the grace of God. In some mysterious way God uses even our sins as silver cords to bind us closer to his son's bleeding side. Even our sins work to our good!

One writer has said that there are no exceptions to the sweeping breadth of Romans 8:28. There is no act of any creature—man, angel, or demon—that cannot ultimately work for our good. No dog can bark or bare his fangs, no man can speak or act against us, no sinister power of evil can conspire to destroy us, but that it *must* work to our good. God has ordained it so.

THE CHRISTIAN OPTIMIST

What conclusions can we draw from this? First, for anyone who believes this verse, suicide would surely be ruled out as impossible—as William Cowper discovered. And not only suicide, but despair, despondency, and discouragement are also ruled out. God, the almighty alchemist, is at work, transforming the lead of our lives into gold. Whatever comes to us will be transformed by the power of God's grace.

Second, this text makes anything but optimism impossible. The Christian *must* be an optimist. He knows that all things are going to work out in the end. Whatever terrible experience you may be going through, even now as you read this chapter—if you can put your faith in God's Word as expressed in this verse, what a weight would be lifted from your shoulders!

Third, Romans 8:28 makes rejoicing required. How can we not praise and rejoice in our God for what he has done for us?

I hope that the incredible sovereignty of God will sift through your mind and heart and will engrave on your consciousness this awesome truth: that God is always working all things together for your good. Rejoice in it!

Let us now look further at the ways God uses adversity to our benefit.

THREE

The Uses of Adversity

Blessed be God ... the Father of mercies, and the God of all comfort; Who comforteth us in all our tribulation, that we may be able to comfort them which are in any trouble, by the comfort wherewith we ourselves are comforted of God. . . . But we had the sentence of death in ourselves, that we should not trust in ourselves, but in God which raiseth the dead: Who delivered us from so great a death, and doth deliver: in whom we trust that he will yet deliver us.

2 Corinthians 1:3-4, 9-10

"SWEET ARE THE USES OF ADVERSITY." So, at least, said Shakespeare. I suspect, however, that if the matter were put to a vote, there would be almost unanimous disagreement with the bard from Stratford-on-Avon. Adversity *sweet*? "Bitter" might be the word. Crushing. Wracking. Wrenching. Faith-shattering. But not sweet.

"WHERE WAS GOD?"

One night I got a phone call from a woman who was an atheist. She called to talk to me—or to talk *at* me—about a long series of tragedies that had taken place in her world, each followed by the complaint, "And where was God *then*?" No doubt you, too, have heard people speak that way. Perhaps you have spoken that way yourself.

I suppose there is nothing that causes more people to stumble in the area of faith than the problem of suffering. None of us is exempt from it. We all face it at one time or another. "Man is born unto trouble," says Scripture, "as the sparks fly upward" (Job 5:7). How true!

"Why, Lord?" "Why me?" Have these words ever echoed through the chambers of your soul in the depths of misery?

REPEAL GRAVITY?

Many people would like to get rid of all pain and trouble and injury and sorrow. But is this what God wants?

Take a simple example. Children fall out of trees and break their arms. People fall from buildings and are killed. We say, "Surely this ought not to be." But shall we therefore repeal the law of gravity?

If we were to do that, it is true that no one would ever again fall from a tree. But is that the kind of world we would want? Where would we be without the law of gravity? Before we rashly tell God what should and should not be, let's think it over for a minute.

Consider your favorite hymn, sung by a magnificent choir. The choir is assisted by the organ, or the piano, or the sound system, or the conductor. But the choir is assisted by the law of gravity more than by any of these. Imagine the conductor trying to lead those folks without gravity. The baritones would be upside down, the sopranos floating amid the trumpets, the altos bouncing off the ceiling. It would be hard to hold the choir together physically, let alone musically. And if you think this picture sounds strange, remember that you would be in precisely the same condition as you listened to that choir!

FAVORITISM AND FINESSE

People get injured and killed in automobile accidents all the time. Shall we then do away with the laws of physics? People are burned with fire. But would we really want fire not to burn? Children touch a hot stove and suffer from the pain. But would we really want to eat plates of raw eggs for breakfast for the rest of our lives?

"Of course not," we say. "That's not the point. We don't want to do away with gravity or physics or heat energy." What we actually want is to do away with what seems like the divine impartiality of it all. We want a world in which fire burns only the bad guys, never the good guys.

But not too openly. Imagine a ball game in which one of the good guys hits a foul ball. At least it *looks* like a foul ball, except the foul line suddenly bends and the ball falls fair. One of the bad guys hits what looks like an obvious home run—except that the outfield fence suddenly recedes so that the ball comes down in the park for a long out. That's not what we want, either. We want God to show some favoritism, but we also want him to use a little finesse!

ME AND MINE

What kind of world would it be if Christians never got sick? If they never fell? Never got burned? Never got into auto accidents? How long would it take for the insurance companies to figure out what was going on?

And how long would it take for other people to catch on? Before long we would have a religion of instant gratification, obvious to everyone. Christians would never go bankrupt. Their kids would never use drugs or run away from home. Their loved ones would never suffer. Do you know what would happen? You would destroy faith. You would destroy character. Religion would become a crass commercial venture (which it already is, for some). Is that what we want?

"No," we say. "I guess not. I guess what I want is not that God would act that way for everyone, all the time. I just want him to do it for *me.*" How many times a day would God hear that pitiful, self-centered appeal? "Just for *me,* Lord. Just for *my* children. Just for *my* friends." Is that what we want? A world that runs on selfishness?

THE RIGHT TO BE UNHAPPY

A world in which there was no pain, no suffering, no danger, and no death would be a world in which there was no adventure. All adventure is built upon danger. There would be no Magellan or Columbus or Balboa. There would be no astronauts going to the moon. Why bother? What would it mean to climb Mount Everest if everyone who fell landed on a cushion of snow?

There would be no challenge. No age-long battle of man against beast, man against the elements, man against disease or poverty or oppression. Literature would be so boring no one would even open a book. All interesting stories are built on conflict. Cowboys and Indians. Cops and robbers. G-men and gangsters.

Do we really want a world in which there is no adventure? No challenge? No conflict? That's the kind of world Aldous Huxley devised in his book, *Brave New World*. It is a world without pain. There is no suffering, no torment, no danger. Someone says, "You have taken away the adventure, the excitement."

The Controller of the brave new world replies proudly, "Yes. This is Christianity without tears."

"But," cries the voice, "the tears are necessary. It's too easy. I want poetry. I want adventure. I want freedom."

"You'll be very unhappy," says the Controller.

"Then," the voice retorts, "I demand the right to be unhappy!"

SORROW AND SYMPATHY

Let's look together at three particular uses of adversity.

First, God uses troubles and sorrows to make us compassionate, and to equip us to comfort others. Paul speaks of this in the passage from 2 Corinthians 1 that opens this chapter. Only those who themselves have passed through the shadow, who have known suffering and trouble, are really able to comfort others.

Years ago a lady in our church had a two-year-old boy who climbed over a fence, fell into a boat canal, and drowned. Our church was quite small at the time, and almost everyone in the church came to visit the woman. As pastor, I stood there in the funeral home parlor throughout, watching the people come and go. The grief-stricken mother told me later that while she appreciated the outpouring of concern, the presence of three people had comforted her most: three other mothers who had also lost young children.

Under the old covenant, when a priest was ordained he had water sprinkled on his head, hands, and feet. Today we who share in the universal priesthood of all believers in the new covenant receive a baptism of tears that equips us for the office of sympathy.

TEARS INTO INK

Where did Paul get the ink to write his comforting epistles? Where did David get the ink to write his psalms of solace? Where did John get the ink to write the tremendously hopeful conclusion to the Book of Revelation? Each of them got the ink from his own tears. When a person has mastered the full curriculum of suffering—completed the course in dungeons and chains, in whips and scourgings, in shipwrecks and persecutions—then that person has received a master's degree in tribulation and is thoroughly qualified for the ministry of compassion.

Think of a seventy-year-old grandmother who has passed through the storms of life. When a young mother who has just lost her child calls at seven in the morning, this older woman knows what to say: she lost a child of her own fifty years ago. At midday she meets a newly-widowed woman who cannot seem to get her feet back on the ground. But she knows the right words: her husband passed away twenty years ago. At midnight she learns of a grandchild who is sick with a fever. She knows how to fluff a pillow, sponge a forehead, give a spoonful of medicine, sing a lullaby. She has done it a thousand times before. She is able to give comfort to others out of the very supply of comfort God has poured out upon her.

GRIEF AND GODLINESS

Second, troubles and sorrows draw us closer to God.

A man was sitting on a train one day and noticed a little girl, about six years old. She was running up and down the aisle, making friends with everyone, laughing, giggling, having a wonderful time. Try as he might, he couldn't tell which of the other passengers on the train she belonged to. She seemed to be able to talk freely with everyone.

Suddenly, the train whistle let out a great shriek, and the train roared into a pitch-dark tunnel. When it came out the other side, there was the little girl cuddled up in the lap of her mother.

How like that child we are! We prance around thoughtlessly as long as the sun is shining and all is well. But when the shriek of trouble comes and the darkness of despair closes in, we remember to whom we belong and throw ourselves into the arms of God.

But trouble doesn't just draw us to God in this life. It also draws us to him for the life hereafter. If we took all the trouble out of life, this world would be a pretty pleasant place to live. Imagine it: no headaches, no financial worries, no nasty neighbors. We might begin to feel that we had all the heaven we needed right here.

But God uses troubles and difficulties to remind us that this world is not all there is. We come to the end of our days thankful for our blessings, but also able to say, "I'm ready to go and be with the Lord. In fact, I'm looking forward to going. I'm ready to leave all this behind and come into my reward."

THE CRUCIBLE

Third, God uses troubles and woes to shape in us the character of Christ. The Bible tells us that Jesus was "a man of sorrows, and acquainted with grief" (Isaiah 53:3). We will never be like Jesus—who was the most perfect person that ever lived—without going through the crucible of suffering.

Someone has said that sorrows humanize the human race. I think it is also true that sorrows Christianize Christians. They make us more like Jesus—if we are yielded to his will.

Often when troubles come upon us we think God is destroying us. Actually, he is tuning us, like a harp. When you tune a harp, you must press it against your shoulder. Sometimes God presses us against his shoulder so that he might tune us, so that we might make more beautiful music for him.

SUFFERERS AND SKEPTICS

It is interesting to note that the great sufferers never become the great skeptics. It is the *spectators* to suffering who become skeptics. It is only in the dark night that you see the star of hope. And the skeptics have not seen it; they have not been in that dark night. They have only stood and watched from a distance. They have seen only the darkness.

Think of Helen Keller, who became blind and deaf in early childhood, for years unable to speak. She said that "the world is full of the overcoming of troubles."

Think of Joni Eareckson, a beautiful young girl paralyzed from the neck down in a diving accident. Out of that tragedy has emerged a faith that has inspired millions.

I will never forget the time, years ago, when Merrill Womack sang at our church. He had crashed his plane in the woods and suffered burns over ninety percent of his body. That would be enough to make most of us shake our fists in anger at God. I will always remember when Merrill sang, "O, how I love him; how I adore him." No, it is the spectators, not the sufferers, who become skeptics.

THE ULTIMATE SOLUTION

The woman who called me that night long ago and recited her litany of sufferings punctuated every item by saying, "Where was God while all this was going on?" The answer is: he was hanging on the cross. The cross is God's ultimate solution to sorrow and suffering. Even now, the

Bible tells us, we are in Christ, and he is in us. Thus all of our pain is in his heart. Our God does not hold himself aloof from our difficulties. He is right here, in the midst of our suffering, enduring more of it than any of us ever has or ever will.

And not only that, but he gives us the power to bear our suffering. He is the God "who delivered us from so great a death, *and doth deliver*" (2 Corinthians 1:10). Regardless of what happens to us in this life, we know that Jesus gives us the strength to bear it.

THE POWER TO OVERCOME

I remember a time in my life when I was going through pain and suffering unlike any I had ever known. At one point I happened to read some words I had seen many times before:

> O love that will not let me go,
>   I rest my weary soul in thee;
> I give thee back the life I owe,
>   That in thine ocean depth its flow
> May richer, fuller, be.

In the midst of the greatest heartache I had ever known, I saw a depth of meaning in those words which, though I had seen them a thousand times before, I had never grasped.

Christ gives us the power to overcome. He has delivered;

he does deliver; he will yet deliver us. Beyond Good Friday lies Easter morning. Beyond the agony of the crucifixion lies the glory of the resurrection. Beyond the sorrow of this vale of tears lies the splendor of paradise. Whatever comes to us, God will enable us to endure it. What a magnificent certainty! How sweet indeed are the uses of adversity!

FOUR

When Troubles Come

As ye have therefore received Christ Jesus the Lord, so walk ye in him. Colossians 2:6

A GREAT PREACHER NAMED JOSEPH PARKER once said that no preacher is so up-to-date as the one who speaks to aching hearts. How true! No one is exempt from trouble. It does not matter whether you are rich or poor, whether you live in a palace or in a shack. Everyone experiences his or her share of hard times. There is not a sheepfold without its missing lamb or a hearth without its empty chair.

Some bear their sorrows silently, while others cry out in the night. Some face trouble with despair, others with hope. Some approach trials in faith, others in the agony of doubt. But all of us face trouble at one time or another. As we have seen from the Book of Job, "Man is born unto trouble, as the sparks fly upward" (Job 5:7).

THE SOURCE OF TROUBLE

I think it is safe to say that every life is shaped, to a large extent, by what it does with the troubles it experiences.

The same problems that produce sinners also produce saints. The way we respond, the way we either open ourselves to God's grace or close our hearts to it, determines the degree to which we allow God to take our troubles and turn them to gold.

How should we respond when troubles come our way? The first thing is to understand *why* they come. In the most general sense, they come because of sin. If there were no sin, there would be no problems in the world. Indeed, there is a day coming when troubles *will* be no more. "Neither shall there be any more pain" (see Revelation 21:4). What a marvelous promise!

Yet it is perhaps too glib simply to say that troubles come because of sin and leave it at that. Any doctor knows it is vital to make as precise a diagnosis as possible, otherwise treatment is made well nigh impossible. Let us look, then, at some of the more particular aspects of trouble.

PREPARING THE WAY

Some troubles are *preparatory*. They clear the way for a greater work of God. When God was preparing the greatest work he was ever to do—sending his Son into the world—there was great trouble on the earth: the slaughter of the innocents at Bethlehem, "Rachel weeping for her children" (Matthew 2:18).

When Jesus came to the consummation of his greatest work—redeeming us on the cross—all hell literally broke loose against him. In earlier times, before the Israelites were delivered from the bondage of Pharaoh, there was the cruelty of the taskmasters and the ten plagues that were visited upon the whole Egyptian people.

Trouble is often the grindstone upon which the axe of battle is sharpened. Billy Graham has often said that when there is great opposition before a crusade, he has learned to anticipate great blessing. I have come to a place in my own life where, when I receive a volley of censure, I simply say, "Well, Lord, I wonder what new opportunities you are planning to open to me now."

THE FURNACE OF AFFLICTION

Trouble is also *educational.* We learn things in the midst of troubles that we do not seem able to learn any other place. I have heard many people come out of the furnace of affliction and say that God spoke to them there, and they heard him there, as they never had before.

It has been well said that the stars come out only at night. Truly we learn lessons in the darkness that we will never learn when the sun is shining brightly and all about us seems bright and peaceful.

A person who has not known trouble and sorrow cannot accomplished anything great. You can see sorrow's touch in the greatest painting; you can hear its tremor in the grandest music; you can sense its power in the finest oratory. The greatest leaders of men are those who have been purified in the furnace of affliction.

THE REAL YOU

Trouble is *revelational.* It reveals a great deal about who we really are inside. When the heat is on, the real person emerges.

The character of Daniel was never more fully revealed than in the glow of the open door of Nebuchadnezzar's furnace. The faith of the apostle Paul was never seen more clearly than in the flash of lightning across the deck of a floundering ship. The courage and faith of the early Christians never stood out more sharply than against the backdrop of the ravenous beasts on the floor of the Roman Colosseum.

Trouble reveals the real you. Amy Carmichael, the poetess, said you can take a glass of clear, pure water and no matter how hard you jostle it, it will never spill a drop of bitter water. Is the water in the vessel of your soul that clear, that pure, that sweet?

INHERITING GOD'S ENEMIES

Trouble is *oppositional.* It is true that when we come to Christ we escape some of the troubles of this world. If we treat our bodies as Scripture urges us—as temples of the Holy Spirit—we greatly lessen our chances of dying of lung cancer or cirrhosis of the liver.

But at the same time, by coming to Christ we invite upon ourselves troubles we would not have known otherwise. Those who look forward to being "carried to the skies on flowery beds of ease" are not reading the same Bible I read! For in God's Word we find it said, "All that will live godly in

Christ Jesus shall suffer persecution" (2 Timothy 3:12).

There are no exceptions. Every man, woman, boy, or girl who has endeavored to be faithful to Jesus Christ, to stand for his cause and to bear his name, has sooner or later gotten pummeled for his efforts!

No one who lives godly in Christ Jesus is exempt. I have heard people say, "I haven't got an enemy in the world." If that is true, then they are no friend of God's! God has a lot of enemies in this world, and all who become his children inherit his enemies.

DRAWING US CLOSER

Finally, troubles sometimes come as *chastisements* from the Lord. The Bible says that every son that the Lord receives, he chastens (see Hebrews 12:6). God's Word tells us we are not to despise the chastening of the Lord, for it will lead to the peaceable fruits of righteousness, even though it is not pleasant at the time.

God uses troubles to draw us closer to himself. We often fail to see the great purpose God has for us. He created us to have fellowship with him. Day in and day out he blesses us in so many ways, yet we so often focus on the gift and overlook the giver. We become spiritually lethargic and forget about God. Some people, it seems, never look up until they are laid flat on their backs.

GETTING OUR ATTENTION

You may remember the old story of the man—new to the ways of the country—who was trying to get his mule into the barn. He was tugging on the rope, pulling with all his might, but the mule wouldn't budge. He got around behind the mule and pushed. He put his shoulder into the animal's hind quarters and leaned his whole weight into the job. But the mule still wouldn't budge.

An old farmer happened along at about that time. He watched the poor man struggle with that obstinate mule for a while, then finally said, "Say, I believe I could get that mule into the barn for you."

"You could?" said the man. "How?"

"Easy," the farmer replied. He picked up a six-foot length of two-by-four wood, walked up to that mule and smashed him right across the bridge of the nose. The mule stood there, dazed and cross-eyed, as the farmer took the rope in his hand and gently led him into the barn.

The man was astonished. "How on earth . . . ?" he stammered.

"Why, mister," the old farmer said, "you know, that old mule is actually a pretty cooperative creature. You've just got to get his attention."

One of the ways God uses trouble is simply to get our attention. When did you last feel God's two-by-four in your life? Did you let God have your undivided attention? We ought to keep in mind that God is all-powerful. If a two-by-four doesn't do the trick, he can be pretty handy with a four-by-six or even an eight-by-twelve!

FELLOWSHIP WITH CHRIST

Of course, we can steer clear of God's two-by-four if we will learn to be attentive to him, to devote our time and energy to developing our relationship with him.

Robert Munger preaches a message called, "My Heart, Christ's Home." It tells of the various "rooms" in the heart of one who has come to know the Lord. One of those rooms is most important. It is a small room, at the bottom of the stairs, just off to the side. That is the room where the Lord says to the new believer, "Here I will meet with you each morning."

Many of us have learned the blessing of making our way to that room, morning after morning, to be with the Lord. To pray. To study his Word in Scripture. Simply to sit and enjoy being in his presence.

But most of us also know that on some mornings we oversleep. We let the pressure of other things detour us from our regular time with the Lord. Day after day we rush down the stairs and out the front door, forgetting about the small room off to the side.

Until one day we notice the door to that room slightly ajar and the light on inside. We peer inside—and there is the Lord, sitting there all alone.

"Lord," we say, "what are *you* doing here?"

"Waiting for you," he replies. "Have you forgotten?"

DRAW NIGH UNTO GOD

What about you? Have you forgotten the room at the bottom of the stairs? God created you for fellowship with himself. Are you enjoying that fellowship? Are you taking advantage of his willingness—his *eagerness*—to spend time with you?

The Scripture says, "Draw nigh to God, and he will draw

nigh to you" (James 4:8). How sad that so many of us have believed the lie of Satan, that if we get too close to God he is somehow going to make our lives miserable. Not so! God wants to bless us. He is a God of love and mercy who delights to bless his children if they will but come to him.

Let me encourage you, as a first step in learning to deal with trouble in your life, to establish a habit of spending time with the Lord each day. I recommend an hour a day. Does that seem like a long time? Studies have shown that the average American family spends more than 35 hours a week watching television. Is one hour a day really too much to give to God?

FIVE CHAPTERS A DAY

Let me also recommend something that many of us have found to be a helpful practice: read five chapters of Scripture each day. It doesn't take that long. The Bible, of course, is really a library of books. I suggest you start with a chapter from one of the historical books of the Old Testament, and then with a chapter from one of the Gospels in the New Testament. Then a chapter from Acts of the Apostles or one of Paul's letters, and finally a chapter apiece from Psalms and Proverbs.

As you read, try each day to find one verse that speaks to your heart in a special way. Spend a few minutes reflecting on it, and let God show you how he means to apply it to your life right now. Mark these verses with a pencil or a felt-tip highlighter so you can refer back to them from time to time. Let God imprint them on your heart. Recite them to yourself during the day. You'll be amazed at how God will enrich your life through his Word.

LOSS OF APPETITE

Do you have a hunger for God? Did you have it once but now find that it has waned? In the natural realm, loss of appetite is a symptom of illness. So it is in the spiritual realm as well. Pray that God will awaken in you a desire for fellowship with him, a hunger for his Word, a longing for his presence. Pray even that he will use his two-by-four, if necessary! Let God use the challenges and difficulties of life to draw you closer to him, to bring you into the fellowship he longs for you to enjoy.

FIVE

Fear Not!

Humble yourselves therefore under the mighty hand of God, that he may exalt you in due time: casting all your care upon him; for he careth for you. 1 Peter 5:6-7

FEAR SEEMS TO BE EPIDEMIC in our society. The Bible said there would be times when men's hearts would fail them for fear, and we appear to be living in just such a time.

Albert Camus, the French existentialist philosopher, called the twentieth century "the century of fear." Perhaps the large amounts of tranquilizers and sleeping pills that Americans take each year confirm that label.

Futurists speculate that by the end of the century the family psychiatrist will have become as common as the family physician. Think of it: every family with its own psychiatrist! Ours is indeed an age of anxiety.

Fear is a debilitating, destructive emotion in the human heart. Where faith strengthens, fear weakens. Where faith liberates, fear imprisons. Where faith empowers, fear paralyzes. Where faith encourages, fear disheartens. Where faith rejoices in its God, fear fills the heart with despair.

Are you fearful? Are you filled with anxieties? Do you lie awake on your bed at night, worried about some nameless dread, something that fills you with disquiet and robs you of sleep? Are you a card-carrying citizen of this century of fear? Let me assure you that even our fears and anxieties can be transformed into gold by the great alchemist.

THE HUMAN CONDITION?

What can be done about this malaise that seems to rest so heavily upon our world—and upon so many of us as individuals? Where does fear come from?

I suppose most people assume that fear of this kind is simply part of the human condition, something that has always been there and always will be. They suppose that not much can be done about it.

Wrong! Studies have shown that it has not always been there—at least not in the forms that seem so epidemic today.

Two sociologists in the 1920's examined a small American town—with the fictitious name of Middletown, though the town itself was real—and found they could not establish a single case of overt anxiety syndrome among the inhabitants.

When Dale Carnegie set out to research his popular book, *How to Stop Worrying and Start Living*, he could not find a single book in the library on the subject. The subject headings in the card catalog jumped straight from "worms" to "worship" without even stopping at "worry."

But before long, things had changed. In 1947 W.H. Auden wrote a poem about the times in which he lived, called "The Age of Anxiety." And, as we have seen, Camus was to describe the twentieth century as "the century of fear." So it seems that the malaise of widespread societal anxiety is a rather recent development in the human condition.

A CHRISTIAN MINDSET

It is astonishing to realize that even during the Middle Ages there is little indication that fear, anxiety, or worry were significant problems. It is astonishing because people then lived under constant threat of plague, famine, flood, and earthquake. The average life expectancy was far shorter than it is now, and "quality of life" as we now think of it was virtually nonexistent. If anyone ever had things to worry about, those people did!

Yet anxiety seems to have been largely unknown. Why? Mainly because the culture operated from a Christian mindset that said God is running the universe, not us. Thus all the events of life, even the difficulties, even the *tragedies*, were seen as coming from God and serving some divine purpose that was beyond our power to know. We could not argue about them, we could not dispute them, we could not justify them. We could only accept them as coming from the hand of a loving—if sometimes mysterious and inscrutable—God. There was no point to worrying about them.

MAN THE MASTER OF ALL THINGS

But with the Renaissance came a new way of thinking. The Renaissance philosophers agreed with Protagoras, the ancient Greek, who said that man was the measure of all things. Well, then, it stood to reason that he should be the *master* of all things as well. Renaissance man believed that the great goal of life was to become the master of one's own environment, one's own circumstances, one's own life. Humankind was to become independent, self-sufficient, and thus aloof from the forces of the cosmos that threatened to engulf and destroy it.

So pervasive has this humanistic way of thinking become that there are very few people who have not imbibed it with their mother's milk and accepted it, uncritically, as the obvious truth. I doubt that there are many people who have not set before their minds, either consciously or unconsciously, the goal of personal independence and self-sufficiency.

THE SHAKY PYRAMID

"Well," you may say, "what is so wrong with that?"

Just this. Christian theologians have always recognized that independence and self-sufficiency are qualities of God. What the Renaissance thinkers bequeathed to us was the notion that human beings are to become their own gods, their own deities.

How was a person's achievement of independence and self-sufficiency to be measured? Why, against the achievements of other independent and self-sufficient people, of course. And since there is only room for one person at the top of the pyramid, the whole world becomes embroiled in a never-ending struggle for place and position, a continual scramble for status and superiority. We begin to seek mastery not only over the impersonal forces of nature, but over each other as well.

The one at the top of the pyramid is never secure, and those at lower levels are never satisfied. Hobbes, the great logician of the Renaissance, said that everyone is a wolf to every other person. Indeed, the whole situation is nothing but the law of the jungle. What a recipe for fear and anxiety on a mass scale!

THE SURPRISING SOLUTION

What is to be done? Many solutions offered for the fears and anxieties that plague modern society are very superficial. They barely scratch the surface. They certainly do not get to the root causes.

But Peter, by the inspiration of the Holy Spirit, gives us the true biblical solution. His words do not stop with the superficial, but cut straight to the heart of the matter. What is the cure for fear? "Humble yourselves therefore under the mighty hand of God, that he may exalt you in due time" (1 Peter 5:6). The solution begins with humility. This is the very opposite of what the Renaissance philosophers prescribed. Rather than try to become gods unto ourselves, we must humble ourselves under the mighty hand of the one true God.

AN END TO MATERIALISM

Scripture also warns each of us "not to think of himself more highly than he ought to think; but to think soberly" (Romans 12:3), recognizing that we are not gods but creatures with various limitations laid upon us by our creator.

This means that our success is not to be measured by our competition with others in the realm of material acquisition. Of course, materialism is virtually the American way of life. We buy cars and houses and boats, and larger cars and houses and boats, not because we need them, but to demonstrate to others (or to ourselves) that we have arrived at a higher level of independence and self-sufficiency—that we have become more like gods.

How different is the standard set by our Lord! He once said, "The foxes have holes, and the birds of the air have nests; but the Son of man hath not where to lay his head" (Matthew 8:20). And this is the one of whom the Father said, "This is my beloved Son, in whom I am well pleased" (Matthew 3:17).

For a Christian, success is not measured against other people, but against the calling and gifts and talents that God has built into him. God has given some people ten talents, some five talents, and others one talent (see Matthew 25:14-30). But the one-talent person need not be frustrated because he cannot "measure up" to the others.

We can be pleasing to God regardless of what we do. If we are using the gifts he gave us to serve his kingdom according to the calling he has placed upon us, and if we are doing it with charity and integrity, then by God's standards we are successful—quite apart from anyone else's accomplishments.

NEVER ALONE

Peter also writes that we are to face difficulties "knowing that the same afflictions are accomplished in your brethren that are in the world. But the God of all grace, who hath called us into his eternal glory by Christ Jesus, after that ye have suffered a while, make you perfect, establish, strengthen, settle you" (1 Peter 5:9-10).

The trials we become so anxious about are universal and inescapable. They happen to all men and women. We are not alone in facing a hostile world—as the Renaissance man supposed. We are never alone! This is our Father's world. Whatever comes to us comes from the hand of our loving and wise Father. We need not receive it in anxiety and fear. We can accept it in faith, knowing that God will use it in his master plan for our lives. The things we are so worried about are the very things God is using to teach us to trust in him.

CASTING CARE AWAY

Peter further tells us that God's people should be "casting all your care upon him; for he careth for you" (see 1 Peter 5:7). In Greek there are two very different words for "care." The first means "cares" in the sense of anxieties.

The other refers to loving concern. We are to cast all our anxieties upon the Lord, who loves us and is concerned for our well-being.

The world tries to tell us, "Don't worry, be happy." It urges us to forget about our cares and just enjoy ourselves. But this approach is psychologically and spiritually dangerous. When we try to pretend that our worries do not exist, in reality we are only repressing them. Working deep within our being, they only become more devastating.

The Bible, however, tells us to bring our worries into the open, look them square in the face, and then cast them upon Christ. The word for "cast" suggests the image of one who has been struggling under a great burden. He has been carrying it for miles and is barely able to take another step. He is staggering, his knees are about to buckle. Then Jesus comes alongside and offers to take the burden off his shoulders. Would he not immediately cast his burden onto Christ? I would!

The next time you find yourself lying awake at night, worrying about this and being anxious about that, recognize that Jesus is right beside you, offering to shoulder the load. Bring your fear into the open and cast it upon him who cares for you.

GOD OUR FATHER

Remember when you were a child? How easy it was, whenever you became frightened, to slip your hand into the hand of your father or mother. All your fears seemed to vanish. Of course, little children grow up, and of necessity become independent of their earthly parents. But how tragic that so many people never discover they have a heavenly Father who is still ready to take their hand in his, onto whom they can cast all their cares.

A missionary was once teaching a recently converted Hindu woman how to pray the Lord's Prayer. "Repeat after me," he said. " 'Our Father . . . .' "

"Just a moment," she interrupted. "Are you speaking of God? Do you mean to tell me that God is my father?"

"That's right," he replied.

"Well, then, that's enough," she said. "If God is my father, there is nothing left to worry about."

Our Father. We have heard those words so many times. But does their full meaning penetrate our soul? Do we understand what that Hindu woman so quickly grasped? If God is our father, there is nothing left to worry about!

"YOU'RE MY DADDY!"

Dr. Harry Ironside tells of a game he used to play with his little son. It was called "Bear." They would arrange a few chairs in the corner and pretend they formed a cage. Then the "bear" would go into the cage. You know, of course, who the "bear" was: it was Papa himself. Papa, on all fours, growls fiercely and raises his "claws" at the little boy, who stands outside laughing at him.

Inevitably, of course, the bear gets out of the cage. Now the game gets exciting! The bear goes after the little boy, who runs for his life, squealing with glee. The father, being on all fours (and perhaps just a tad overweight), has some difficulty catching the youngster. But eventually he manuevers him into a corner.

Trapped, the little boy puts his arms over his face and begins to scream with excitement and fear. He knows the vicious "bear" is upon him. He can hear the growling and feel the hot breath on his arms. Any moment, the bear's claws will reach out and grab him and he will be devoured!

Then suddenly the little boy whirls around, throws his arms around the "bear," and says, "I'm not scared! I know you're not a bear! You're my daddy!"

So many people think God is a great cosmic bear, out to destroy them. When we are able to see that he is a loving father, when we can throw ourselves into his arms, when we can say, "You're my daddy!"—then fear will fade away. Then we can sing the lovely hymn,

> *This is my Father's world,*
> *I rest me in the thought.*

Now that we have begun to understand how God helps us deal with the basic problem of fear, let's look at some closely related problems that often come upon us: discouragement and worry.

SIX

How to Deal with Discouragement

But he himself went a day's journey into the wilderness, and came and sat down under a juniper tree: and he requested for himself that he might die; and said, It is enough; now, O LORD, take away my life; for I am not better than my fathers.
1 Kings 19:4

A PREACHER ONCE SAID he had learned that he needed to select his sermon topics with care. Whenever he planned to preach on a problem, and especially on how to solve it, it seemed the Lord always gave him an extra dose of that problem the week before. It was as though the Lord wanted to give him an opportunity to "road test" his solution before he gave it to his congregation!

Apparently it is the same with authors. Little did I know, when I set out to write about discouragement, what a depressing week I would have! Every day, it seemed, one more discouraging piece of news would come my way from some quarter. I felt like a tent peg being slowly hammered into the ground.

I'm not alone. Experts say depression has reached epidemic proportions in our society. At any given moment, they say, as many as twenty percent of the people in the United States are experiencing some form of depression. That amounts to as many as fifty million people!

CHARLIE BROWN

Defeat comes at us from all directions. Your daughter comes home from school and tells you she didn't make the school band. Your son pitches his first Little League game and gives up nine runs in the first inning.

People get depressed because they are lonely. All the mail in their mailbox is addressed to "Occupant." They suffer from the Rodney Dangerfield syndrome: they "don't get no respect." Their name has never become a household word, even in their own household! They feel, as George Goebel used to say, as if "the world were a tuxedo and they were a pair of brown shoes."

We all occasionally feel like Charlie Brown, of the "Peanuts" cartoon strip. Charlie has his own personal, private critic. Lucy is always on hand, always ready to tell him in excruciating detail just what a loser he is. "You, Charlie Brown, are a foul ball in the line drive of life. You're a miscue! You're three putts on the eighteenth green! You're a seven-ten split in the tenth frame! You're a dropped rod and reel in the lake of life! You're a missed free throw, a shanked nine-iron, a called third strike! Have I made myself clear?"

Yes, indeed. Lucy manages to make herself very clear

indeed. Maybe you know a Lucy. Maybe you are married to a Lucy. Maybe your spouse is married to a Lucy! Some of us don't even need a Lucy; we are very adept at running ourselves down with a constant stream of self-criticism.

HOPE DEFERRED

Discouragement, one way or another, comes to all of us. Even the great giants of faith, like the prophet Elijah, have had times of discouragement. After the greatest triumph of his life, when he has taken on the entire corps of prophets of the false god Baal and destroyed them all, Elijah flees for his life at the threat of the wicked queen, Jezebel. "It is enough," he cries out. "Now, O LORD, take away my life" (1 Kings 19:4).

Have you ever felt like that? Persecution can certainly produce discouragement. The apostle Paul often felt it. He was pressed down, he was persecuted, he was brought almost to the point of death. Yet he found strength amidst his trials as he looked to Jesus Christ, in whom he found the perfect antidote for discouragement.

We can become discouraged when our dreams are dashed, when our expectations are not realized. "Hope deferred maketh the heart sick," Scripture says (Proverbs 13:12). Something we have waited for, looked for, longed for, simply does not materialize. We have prayed for it, perhaps for years, yet it has not happened.

Abraham experienced this kind of discouragement. God had promised to raise up a great nation through him. Yet for years he had no offspring. Finally he lamented, "What wilt though give me, seeing I go childless? ... Behold, to me thou hast given no seed" (Genesis 15:2, 3). Yet God did hear his prayer, and answered it in his own perfect timing, and drew Abraham out of the pit of despondency.

BARBS OF CRITICISM

As our friend Lucy has demonstrated, criticism can be a devastating source of discouragement. When Rachmaninoff, the great composer, performed his first symphony, it was met with such a storm of criticism from the music world that he suffered an almost total emotional breakdown. He would have given up had it not been for a doctor friend who took him into his house and cared for him. Rachmaninoff went on to produce some of the most magnificent music ever composed.

Thomas Hardy, one of the greats of British literature, was so distraught over criticism of his novels that he gave up his writing career. It is tragic to think how much more he might have given to the world were he not devastated by criticism.

Author and speaker Zig Ziglar has pointed out that no one has ever erected a statue to a critic. Yet every person who attempts to do anything worthwhile in life can count on feeling the barbs that the inevitable critics will throw his way.

Robert G. Lee tells the story of a depressed man who went to see a psychiatrist for help. The doctor suggested he read a novel; perhaps the distraction might be helpful. The man said no, thank you, he didn't care for novels. The doctor then suggested that he go to the theatre; perhaps that might lift his spirits. No, the man said gloomily, he didn't think that would help either.

Finally the doctor said, "I can only think of one other person who might be able to help you. Go and see that great clown who has just arrived in town and is drawing such great crowds."

"Ah, doctor," the man sighed. "I *am* that clown!"

He expressed what you and I know only too well; when we are caught in the icy grip of discouragement, the last person who can help us escape is ourself!

THE SURE CURE

Can even the base metal of discouragement be turned to gold by God's grace? Certainly! The sure cure for discouragement is faith in God's Word. He tells us that whatever comes to us comes through his love and that he will make it work for our good. He promises that he will deliver us after we have suffered for a little while. He tells us that he is bringing us through the fires of affliction so that what is dross in our lives can be purged and what is gold can be refined.

After all, what is a precious gem but a mere piece of earth that has survived the trauma of severe heat and pressure? In the struggles of our life, God seeks only to make us jewels for his crown. Instead of wearing us down, the grindstone of life can polish us up if we embrace its work with faith in God. If we are trusting in Christ to take us and make us into what he would have us be, then we can find our comfort in him no matter how discouraging our circumstances.

THE MINORITY REPORT

Someone has said that the world can be divided into two groups of people: those who believe the world can be divided into two groups, and those who do not!

But seriously, there is a great divide between people who are *discouragers* and those who are *encouragers*.

How many people there are who will always be glad to tell you that whatever it is you are trying to do will never work. They know a hundred and one reasons why something cannot possibly succeed. "You don't have it in you." "It's just not meant to be—for you." "You ought to just give up."

I am reminded of the biblical stories of the twelve spies who went into the land of Canaan to reconnoiter the land for the people of Israel. When they returned, ten of them joined to give the majority report: "The people is greater and taller than we; the cities are great and walled up to heaven; and moreover we have seen the sons of the Anakims there" (Deuteronomy 1:28). The Anakim were giants. Goliath was one of their number.

But there was also a minority report. Joshua and Caleb, God's intrepid heroes, God's men of faith, stepped forward and said, "We are well able to overcome it" (Numbers 13:30). We may indeed be as grasshoppers in the eyes of our foes, they said. But the Lord will give us victory!

Strengthened by Joshua's and Caleb's words, the

Israelites went out to fight their "unconquerable foe." And God did indeed make them victorious.

SONS OF ENCOURAGEMENT

There is something wonderful about encouragers—people who, instead of robbing us of hope and courage, actually impart strength to us.

In the New Testament we read of Barnabas, one of the most prominent encouragers in the Bible. His original name was Joseph, but because of his characteristic ability to strengthen and build up other people, he was given the name Barnabas, which literally means "Son of Encouragement."

When the new Christians were refusing to accept Paul—who after all had just been converted from being the vicious persecutor, Saul—it was Barnabas who took him in, encouraged him to keep going, and encouraged the church leaders to give him a hearing.

When the church in Jerusalem was suffering financially, it was Barnabas who came to their aid, selling his farm and laying the money at the apostles' feet.

When Paul angrily dismissed Mark from his mission team, it was Barnabas who encouraged Mark not to give up, and even joined with him in a mission to Cyprus.

Barnabas' encouragement, which kept Mark from being overwhelmed by his earlier failure, ultimately enabled him to rise up and accomplish great things for the kingdom of God. He gave us the indispensable Gospel of Mark. Indeed, late in life Paul himself was to say of him, "Take Mark, and bring him with thee: for he is profitable to me for the ministry" (2 Timothy 4:11).

HOW TO "BE SOMEBODY"

All of us, at some level of our being, want to "be somebody," to "make something of ourselves." We want to accomplish some great achievement, attain recognition for some form of expertise, live the lifestyle of the rich and famous. Most of all, perhaps, we want to be remembered as someone who did great things for God.

We know, of course, that such things may or may not come our way. We may not be the next Paul. We may not become famous. We may honestly feel that we don't really have that much to offer the world.

But let me tell you something. No matter what else does or does not come to pass in your life, there is a way you can make a lasting difference in your world. I want to challenge you to become an encourager, to become one who by his words and deeds builds others up rather than tears them down, who imparts hope and determination rather than despair.

"GOD LIVES!"

Martin Luther had times of almost overwhelming discouragement in his life. During one of those periods, his wife came into his study. She was dressed in black mourning garments. Luther asked, "Why are you dressed all in black?"

"Because," she replied, "God is dead."

"Nonsense, woman," Luther snapped. "God lives!"

"If you believe that," she replied, "then act like it! Live like it!"

I am grateful to God that my own wife is an encourager. She rallies to my side in times of need. I pray that God will place an encourager in your life. More than that, I pray that he will make *you* an encourager in the lives of others.

If you would be loved by other people, become an encourager. If you would make a contribution, even when you think you have nothing to offer, become an encourager. If you would like to see your family, your office, your organization, your church, grow and thrive, become an encourager. Those around you already have enough people to tell them what *can't* be done. Why not decide to become a person who encourages them with what *can* be done?

BELIEVING GOD'S PROMISES

To be an encourager requires only that you be a person of faith. An encourager is simply one who believes God's promises: that he will never leave us or forsake us; that he will work all things together for our good; that he will grant us victory as we trust in him.

We have those promises safely and securely in God's Word. Let's claim them! Let's believe them! Let's share them with others and become one of those most important of people: encouragers. As we do, we will lighten the loads and lift the hearts of many. We will chase away the dark clouds of despair and bring in the sunshine of hope. We will help others—and, in the process, help ourselves—throw off the weight of discouragement.

SEVEN

God's Cure for Anxiety

Be careful for nothing; but in every thing by prayer and
supplication with thanksgiving let your requests be made
known unto God. Philippians 4:6

A S WE HAVE SEEN, ours has very appropriately been called
the Age of Anxiety. We had thought that by con-
quering the forces of nature and bending them to the will of
man, we would deliver ourselves from our problems and
enter a golden age.

Unfortunately, it did not work out that way. Instead, like
Dr. Frankenstein, we have created a monster. Dr. Frankenstein intended his creature to be helpful. But it went wild.
The creature terrorized his life and the lives of others, and
finally drove him to a horrible end. So it is with the powers
of our world today. They have, indeed, been harnessed. But
unfortunately they have been harnessed unto our destruction as well as unto our good.

Thus society seems overcast by a cloud of dread.
Psychiatrists call it *angst*—an unspecified, undesignated,
unnamed fear that hovers over everything.

WORRY IS A SIN!

Are you a worrier? Do you feel that you just have to worry about things?

Well, of course! you say. Look at the times we live in. There are terrible things going on out there. Ominous clouds loom on the horizon. What person in his right mind would *not* be worried in times like these?

Are you a worrier? Some people are not the least bit hesitant to admit it. They'll tell you, "Oh, I'm just a worry-wart." They see it as a basic component of their identity.

It has always struck me as odd that even Christians act this way. Do you know that the Bible treats worry as a sin? It does! Now, what good church-going person would ever smile, look you in the eye, and say, "Well, you know me, I'm just an adulterer?" Or, "Oh, I've just always been a murderer?" But they *will* say, "I'm a worrier," which is just another particular way of proclaiming, "I'm a sinner."

Worry is a sin for at least three reasons.

First, worry accomplishes nothing good. Absolutely nothing. You can worry yourself into a peptic ulcer, and that airplane is not going to land one minute sooner than if you hadn't worried at all. That train won't arrive one hour sooner. Your daughter is not going to come home one moment sooner. Worry does not accomplish anything good. It just grinds down the machinery.

Second, worry *does* accomplish some things that are bad. It destroys the human body, which Scripture tells us is the temple of the Holy Spirit. Doctors can give us a long list of problems that are either caused, or made worse, by worry:

fatigue, headaches, arthritis, rheumatism, ulcers, digestive disorders, nervous breakdown—the list goes on and on.

"GOD, THOU LIEST!"

Third, and most basically, worry is a sin because at heart it is nothing less than disbelief in God. It is simply unbelief coiled at the core of your soul, poised to strike and inject poison into your life.

John Haggai has said, "God's Word says, 'Cast all thy cares on him, for he cares for thee,' but worry says, 'God, thou liest!' God's Word says, 'Thy God shall supply all thy needs out of his riches in glory,' but worry says, 'God, thou liest!' God's Word says he will work all things together for good, but worry says, 'God, thou liest!' "

Worry is an expression of unbelief. Faith and worry cannot coexist in the same person, about the same thing, at the same time. One inevitably drives out the other. To the degree that you are worried about something, you are not trusting God for it, and vice versa. That is why worry is a sin.

ROBBED OF JOY

Some people believe that the things they are worried about are "crosses" God has called them to bear. But the fact is that when God gives us a cross to bear, he also gives us the grace to bear it in faith. When we manufacture crosses for ourselves, out of our own fears and anxieties, they bring no grace with them at all. Rather they bring a faithless spirit that shuts out grace and makes everything more difficult, distasteful, unendurable.

Worry robs life of its joy. One thing is certain: a person who is a worrier will never fulfill Scripture's charge to us that says, "Rejoice in the Lord alway: and again I say, Rejoice" (Philippians 4:4). This the worrier cannot do. Joy cannot coexist with worry any more than faith can.

ANXIOUS FOR NOTHING

The Scripture says, "Be careful for nothing" (Philippians 4:6). The word "careful" in this case means just what its component parts signify: "full of care." Today we might say "careworn," or, more simply, "anxious." The verse is a commandment. It tells us, "Do not be worried about anything."

Well, you say, surely the person who made this statement knew nothing of the kinds of problems that *I* face in *my* life!

Guess again! The man who wrote these words was the apostle Paul. He wrote them from a dungeon in Rome, where he had been imprisoned for preaching the gospel of Christ. He was facing the prospect of a trial before the emperor Nero. Nero was a great lover of truth and light, of course. We know he was a lover of light because he used to enjoy covering Christians with tar, tying them to poles, setting them on fire, and lighting his garden with them!

Paul knew his prospects were grim. Ahead of him lay

only calamity. Yet, even from the dungeon, he could encourage us, "Be anxious for nothing!" Paul knew, as one writer said, that when Rome fixed its claws it never let go until it had drawn blood. Yet he could say, "Rejoice in the Lord!"

"Be anxious for nothing." The emphasis, I believe, is on the word *nothing*. Paul does not say, "Be anxious about only one or two things," or, "Be anxious about as few things as possible." No, he says, "Be anxious about *nothing*."

Are you a transgressor of this commandment? So am I, all too often. But to the degree that we do transgress this commandment, we suffer for it. God doesn't want that for you or for me.

SAND IN THE GEARS

John Haggai tells of how he suffered for his worrying as a young man. He had a nervous breakdown while he was still in his twenties. At the time he was carrying nineteen semester hours in college, pastoring his first church, and conducting evangelistic crusades in his "spare time." John estimates he was regularly working close to ninety hours per week.

Everyone, he says, felt sorry for him. His teachers in school felt sorry for him. His parishioners felt sorry for him. The people connected with the evangelistic crusades felt sorry for him. But nobody felt more sorry for him than he did for himself!

In simple fact, John was miserable. He had lost all joy. He had poured sand into the gears of his motor and it was running rough! Before long it broke down completely, and he was sent away for a rest cure. During that time he discovered God's cure for worry. Since then, he says, he has never lost five minutes' sleep to anxiety.

GOD'S CURE FOR WORRY

There is a cure for worry! In the same verse in which God gives us the prohibition against worry, he also gives us the divine prescription for its cure. "Be careful for nothing," he says, "but in everything by prayer and supplication with thanksgiving let your requests be made known unto God."

The word translated "careful," or "full of care," is *mermnao*, which comes from a root word which means "a divided mind." It speaks of a mind that endlessly bats things back and forth and cannot decide what to do. It just keeps chasing problems back and forth until finally the mechanism simply wears out.

As I was studying for this chapter, a problem suddenly leapt over the top of my desk and plopped itself down on my book, blotting everything else from view. It was a very serious problem. There it was, just sitting there, pulsating, screaming for my attention.

Being an obedient servant of the "god of worry," I picked it up and began to play mental ping-pong with it. Back and forth in my mind it went. Of course, this accomplished nothing. I only made me dizzy! But after a couple pings and pongs I remembered what I was studying, and the next time it came by I bounced it right up to God! I committed the problem to his care and asked him to provide what was needed. I thanked him for his mercy in being willing to answer my prayer, and I thanked him for what I knew he would do on my behalf.

The result? That pulsating problem just disappeared! I had peace, and was able to go back to studying. *Believing prayer, marked by supplication and thankfulness, that is God's cure for worry.*

THE PRIVILEGE OF PRAYER

Believing prayer! How often do we think of prayer as a burden, a duty, rather than as an inestimable privilege— the privilege of casting all our cares upon the Lord and placing our trust in him? Prayer can be a tremendous source of strength and refreshment, if we will but learn to cast our burdens upon the Lord and wait upon him. When we do, we enter into the peace "which passeth all understanding," which "shall keep our hearts and minds through Christ Jesus" (see Philippians 4:7).

I recently saw a television commercial that illustrated our modern problem. A car had been rigged up with two seats on the outside of the car. One was connected directly to the front wheel, and the other was connected to the frame of the car. A dummy was placed in each seat and the car was sent rolling along a railroad bed.

As you can well imagine, the front wheels were bouncing up and down frantically, and the dummy in the seat connected to those front wheels was getting a pretty wild ride. The dummy in the other seat was riding serenely along without so much as being jostled. Why? Because his seat was connected to the frame, which had shock absorbers to cushion the impact of the railroad tracks. The question is, which kind of dummy are you?

GOD'S SHOCK ABSORBER

Believing prayer is God's shock absorber for our lives. It enables us to move tranquilly through life without the bumps and bruises that come from distrusting the promises of God.

How many people miss this marvelous provision of God! They grab hold of some earthly, finite thing and hold onto it tenaciously. Even when the ride gets bumpy, they hang on. They try to provide for themselves because they do not trust God to take care of them.

The famous Dr. Kidd, a great preacher from Aberdeen, Scotland, was talking to some of the young men who worked with him in the church. He told them he had experienced good success with the major issues of life. God had helped him deal with them victoriously. No, he said, it was the little irritations of life that seemed to overcome him, to cause him to say and do things he later regretted. One of the young men suggested that perhaps Dr. Kidd was committing the big things to God, but trying to handle the little things by himself. Is this not true of so many of us? Be they great or small, when we try to handle things without God, we inevitably fail.

A LIFE OF SERENITY

Someone has said, "We are able to be careful for nothing because we know that our God is careful for everything." How true! Our God cares for us! Perhaps you have never believed it possible that you could live a life of serenity in the midst of all the problems of life. But you can. How? In everything—not just in some things, not just in a few things, but in *everything*—let your requests be made known to God by prayer and supplication with thanksgiving. This is God's cure for worry. Couldn't you stand to take a dose of it right now?

EIGHT

I Refuse to Worry!

Therefore I say unto you, Take no thought for your life, what ye shall eat, or what ye shall drink; nor yet for your body, what ye shall put on. Is not the life more than meat, and the body than raiment? Behold the fowls of the air: for they sow not, neither do they reap, nor gather into barns; yet your heavenly Father feedeth them. Are ye not much better than they? **Matthew 6:25-26**

I T WAS ALMOST THIRTY YEARS AGO. I had been a Christian for only a month or so, and I was filled with love for all mankind—the classic Good Samaritan. A fellow employee called me from the hospital. She had just undergone an emergency appendectomy, she said, and she needed to talk with me. I went to see her, my imagination filled with thoughts of the marvelous spiritual consolation I was going to bring her.

When I got to her bedside, it turned out that what she really wanted was three hundred dollars to pay her bill so she could get out of the hospital! I didn't have that kind of money. But, convinced it was my spiritual duty to do what

I could as a Good Samaritan, I decided to borrow the money in my own name and help this damsel in distress. I took out a loan at a local finance company—at a very high rate of interest, I might add—and bailed her out.

She had promised that I could have her car as collateral against the loan, but I had waved her off. "No, no," I said, "Don't be ridiculous. I trust you." But the minute she got out of the hospital she suddenly seemed to lose her memory concerning the money she owed me. Before long it became clear she had no intention of ever paying me back. I was left with the task of paying off the loan, and the exorbitant interest, myself. It was a bitter but worthwhile lesson for me.

HOW WORRY "WORKS"

Suppose for a moment I told you that I was still paying the interest on that long-ago loan—indeed, that I had been paying nothing *but* interest all these years, and had never made a dent in the principal. As a result, I now owed even more money to the finance company than I did when I started out—even though I'd been paying on it for thirty years.

Now suppose you said to me, "That's absurd. Why on earth did you ever borrow the money in the first place?" and I replied, "Well, to tell you the truth, I never actually *did* borrow any money. I'm just paying interest." Would you not think me more than a little foolish? To spend all these years paying interest on a loan I never even received? Surely you would consider me one of the greatest fools you had ever met! And you would be absolutely right.

Here is the point of my story: worry works exactly the same way. Haven't you spent a good many hours of your life worrying about things that never came to pass? Weren't you then doing nothing more than paying interest on a debt you did not owe in the first place? And even if the thing you worried about *did* come to pass, did your worrying make it any better? Were you not then merely paying interest without touching the principal?

We all know the story of the young lad out stalking the back yard with pith helmet and safari rifle, erecting a bizarre contraption of ropes, saplings, and nets. A neighbor asked him, "What's that for?"

"To keep wild elephants away," the boy replied soberly.

"But that's silly," said the neighbor. "There aren't any wild elephants within a thousand miles of here."

"You see?" cried the lad. "It works!"

Many people will tell you that worry "works" in just this same way. "Don't tell me worry is a waste of time," they say. "Why, I've been worrying for years about all kinds of awful things, and not one of them has happened yet!"

WHEN TO CROSS THE RIVER

Shortly after he was elected president, Abraham Lincoln stopped in New York on his way to Washington to meet with the famous newspaperman, Horace Greeley. Greeley asked the question that was on everyone's mind at the time: Are we going to have a civil war?

Lincoln answered, as he so often did, by telling a story. He told of the days when he was a circuit-riding lawyer. He would travel to all the small towns throughout the region, wherever court was being held. This of course involved frequent river crossings, particularly of the notorious Fox River, turbulent and very dangerous in times of heavy rain.

On one occasion, after crossing several rivers with no small amount of difficulty, Lincoln's companion shook his head and said, "If these rivers are this bad, whatever will it be like when we must cross the Fox?" As it happened, that night they met an itinerant Methodist minister at the inn where they were staying. They asked if he knew the Fox River. "Oh, yes," the preacher said. "I know it well. I have crossed it innumerable times these many long years." They asked if he had any advice about how they might cross it safely.

"Absolutely!" he grinned. "I have discovered a secret about crossing the Fox River which I never fail to keep in mind. It is this: I never cross the Fox River until I *reach* the Fox River. Good night, gentlemen."

How much time and energy have you and I wasted crossing rivers we had not even come to yet—and then finding, when we did come to them, that they had become merely dry river beds that were easily crossed? We could learn from the experience of another president, Calvin Coolidge. He said, "When you see ten troubles coming down the road, you can be sure that nine of them will run into the ditch before they reach you." So why worry about them?

THE WORRY OF WAITING

Thomas Carlyle, a brilliant writer, suffered greatly from worry. Should you tour his home in the Chelsea section of

London, England, you would be shown a special chamber where he slept and did his writing. It was soundproofed so the noise of the busy street outside would not disturb his concentration.

For some reason, however, the soundproofing was not adequate to keep out the crowing of his neighbor's rooster. This drove him to distraction, so much so that he finally complained to his neighbor who replied, "Well, he only crows three times a night. I should not think that would be such a terrible distraction." Carlyle exclaimed, "Oh, but if you only knew how much I suffer *waiting* for that cock to crow!" How much agony do we put ourselves through, anxiously anticipating things that may never even happen!

THE GRAY SISTER OF CARE

There is an interesting passage in Goethe's *Faust* that helps us understand the nature of worry. Four gray sisters appear at the door of the palace where Faust is staying. They are Want, Guilt, Necessity, and Care. The first three cannot find entrance. But the last gray sister, Care—or Worry—makes her way in through the keyhole. She says to Faust:

> Whom I possess shall never
>   Find the world worth his endeavor.
> Endless gloom around him folding,
>   Rise nor set of sun beholding,
> And he knows not how to measure
>   True possession of his treasure.
> Be in happiness or sorrow,

He postpones it 'til the morrow:
To the future only cleaveth,
   Nothing, therefore, he achieveth.

Having said these words, Care breathes into the face of Faust and he is struck blind.

I wonder how many of us have been blinded by the corroding effects of worry and care, blinded to the joys and happiness of life, such that all serenity has been taken from us.

STRANGLED BY WORRY

What a useless thing it is to worry!

That does not mean we are not to give proper forethought to our lives, or to do prudent planning. It does, however, mean there is no point to endlessly going over things which we cannot, at the moment, do anything about. We all know those times when worry turns our bed into a rack of pain. Worry, as we have seen, never does anything useful.

The words "worry" and "anxiety" are derived, respectively, from the Latin and Anglo-Saxon forms of a root word that means "to choke" or "to strangle." And that, of course, is what worry does. It chokes us. Have we not often said, when a burden that was causing us to worry has suddenly been lifted, "Now I can breathe easier?" Worry deprives us of the breath of life and the joys that come with it.

Worry not only robs our mind of peace, it also robs our

body of health. One physician has said that there are innumerable people whose cause of death could have been listed simply as worry. A doctor at the Mayo Clinic once said that eighty percent of stomach disorders were directly traceable to anxiety. He said faith was more important than food when it came to curing ulcers.

The French word *sabot* refers to a wooden shoe. The familiar word "sabotage" is derived from it. It seems some Dutchmen found that an effective way to disrupt work at French manufacturing plants was by tossing their wooden shoes into the machinery. Worry is like a wooden shoe cast into the machinery of our being. It disrupts the work of our mind and destroys the machinery of our body.

TURNING BLESSINGS INTO CURSES

Worry is also harmful to the spiritual life. Jesus observed that the cares of this world could choke out the good seed of God's Word and prevent it from taking root and bearing fruit in our lives.

Indeed, the cares of this world prevent some people from entering the kingdom of God in the first place. I remember talking to a person I dearly loved about the kingdom of God and the salvation offered to us in Christ. He cut me short by telling me he had so many problems and worries that he did not have time or inclination to even think about what I was saying to him. If this is true for the unbeliever, it is often true for the believer as well: the cares of this world keep us from being fruitful for Christ.

In the last chapter we saw that worry was a sin because it

sprang from unbelief. But worry is also sinful because it cuts us off from the help God wants to give us. Worry is, in effect, taking upon ourselves responsibilities that properly belong on God's job description, not ours.

Worry is also a sin because it corrupts our view of the blessings of God. Someone has said that many of our cares represent nothing more than a morbid way of looking at our privileges. How many people worry about the very job they once prayed God would give them? How many lose sleep trying to figure out how they are going to get by on "only" $100,000 a year? How many times do we comment on the anxieties that come our way because of our children—surely among God's greatest blessings to us? Thanks to worry, all these blessings begin to seem like curses.

SHOULD YOU WORRY?

I sometimes like to say that the only people in this world who really need to worry are those who have not committed their lives to Christ. God's command *not* to worry, and his marvelous promises that make worry a waste of time, are given only to his children, to those who have trusted Christ as their savior. The only reason we can be free of worry is because Christ has taken away the guilt of our sins, he has taken upon himself the punishment that hangs over all our heads.

Those who have never surrendered their lives to Christ ought actually to worry more than they do. They are the ones who really have something to worry about! If they knew what awaited them in the next life, I think un-believers would worry a lot more than they do. Now they may worry about going financially bankrupt; in reality they should worry about going spiritually bankrupt. It is one thing to spend the rest of this life in the poorhouse; it is quite another to spend the next life in hell!

If you do not know Jesus Christ as your personal Lord and Savior, I pray you will let worry drive you to the cross. There on your knees before him, dump the burden of sin upon Jesus so that he may bear it for you. Then you can lay upon him your burden of care as well.

JUST SAY NO

For those who *do* know Christ, the way to handle worry is simply to refuse to do it! Too many of us walk around like Atlas, carrying the weight of the world on our shoulders, not realizing that God wants us to simply shrug it off and leave it to him. Take the weight of worry that burdens you and cast it onto Christ.

Then refuse to take it back! When the devil says to you, "You'd better worry about this; lay awake nights turning it over and over in your mind"—just say no!

The phenomenal truth is that God does not want us to worry, and we do not have to! God wants us to rejoice. He wants us to come to him with believing prayer, in supplication with thanksgiving, letting all our requests be made known to God, casting our cares upon him who cares for us.

God provides everything necessary so that we do not *have* to worry. He even commands us not to worry! I, for one, have made up my mind: I refuse to worry. How about you?

NINE

On the Leaping of Walls

For by thee I have run through a troop: by my God have I leaped over a wall. **2 Samuel 22:30**

NOT LONG AGO I SAW A BOOK ENTITLED, *Not Made for Defeat.* That is a great truth which, I suspect, most of us have never really grasped. You and I, who belong to the living God, have not been made for defeat. We have been made to conquer!

How well the apostle Paul put it when he said that Christ always leads us forth in triumphal procession (see 2 Corinthians 2:14). The image is of a Roman general returning from battle, leading his vanquished foe through the streets of the city.

Christ always leads us forth in triumph: we simply are not made for defeat. Why is it then, that so many Christians seem so defeated so much of the time? I believe it is because they have never learned the secret of "running through troops" and "leaping over walls," as David put it in 2 Samuel. These are important ways in which we cooperate with the divine alchemist as he takes our problems and turns them to gold.

THE SECRET

The secret of leaping walls, simply put, is *faith*.

Now we already know that it is by faith in the crucified and risen Christ that men and women are redeemed, forgiven, and granted eternal life. Paradise is already paid for; it is offered freely to those who trust in Christ.

Faith is the only ship that sails for paradise. It is the only key to the mansions above, which Christ has gone ahead to prepare for those who are his own. Faith is the pillow on which we lay our heads at the last.

Many of us have grasped this great truth but have failed to grasp its corollary. Faith is not only that by which we *die*, it is also that by which we *live*. It is by faith that we overcome the myriad trials and temptations that confront us daily in this life. It is by faith that we "overcome the world" (John 6:33). It is by faith that we conquer. It is by faith that we run through troops and leap over walls.

THE PRISON OF IMPOSSIBILITY

"Running through troops" and "leaping over walls" are simply poetic descriptions of experiences familiar to everyone. We have all faced what seemed at the time to be insurmountable obstacles—as though Satan gathered the bricks of circumstance and built a mighty prison of impossibility around us. With one brick of discouragement after another, he walled us in until there seemed to be no way out. Overwhelming temptation, physical disablement, financial disaster, family turmoil—all of them have been bricks that Satan has used to hem us in.

If you find yourself behind such a wall today, let the psalmist's proclamation pierce your soul: *"By my God have I leaped over a wall."*

Notice that David's words contain no vain boasting, no humanistic self-conceit. "It is *by my God,"* he says, "that I have done this." David knew the divine principle: "Cursed be the man that trusteth in man, and maketh flesh his arm" (Jeremiah 17:5). Even as a young shepherd boy facing battle with the giant Goliath, did not David declare that he relied not on his own strength but on the strength of "the LORD of hosts, the God of the armies of Israel" (see 1 Samuel 17:45-47)?

How the Bible lashes out at the scornful, the self-confident, the self-important, those who suppose themselves to be something. The Pharaohs in their opulent palaces. The Nebuchadnezzars strutting upon the roofs of their palaces, vainly declaring their majesty over the city of Babylon. Jezebel boasting of her power and beauty. Each and every one trips over pride and plunges headlong into the pit of perdition.

David trusted not in himself, but only in the living God! He believed that God would "light his lamp" when the darkness of circumstances crowded in on him and made the future look bleak indeed (see 2 Samuel 22:29). David declared, "I know God will help me."

SOUNDING THE TRUMPET

How did David know this? Because he knew God had helped him in the past. "For by thee *I have run* through a troop: by my God *have I leaped* over a wall." Remembrance of past victories by the grace of God were, for David, a stimulus to courage in the face of new problems and difficulties.

How about you? Have you not known God's deliverance in the past—perhaps dozens or even hundreds of times? Will you now lie down and die of despair because of some new problem that threatens to engulf you? Who is the troop that comes against you now? What is the wall that Satan would build around you now? Sound the trumpet of faith! Let the drums roll and the banners fly, and watch that wall crumble as at Jericho! Then leap over the ruins!

Are you a leaper and a runner? Or are you a crawler and a flopper? Some people face not a troop, but only a solitary adversary who may turn out to be a mere shadow even at that. But they cry out, "There is a lion in the street," and run for cover. When David leaped over that wall, it was an offensive maneuver, not a defensive one. We are likewise called to go on the attack, not just to hunker down and hope to wait out the storm.

LINKED TO GOD'S POWER

Tragically, there are many Christians who do not realize the great power that is available to them. Remember the words of the hymn, "I link my earthly feebleness to thy almighty power." Is this not a good definition of Christianity? That is precisely the claim that Christianity makes—to link weak men and women to the divine power of God. That claim is substantiated by the parting promise of Jesus Christ: "Ye shall receive power" (Acts 1:8).

Power! In the Greek it is *dunamis,* from which we get our English word "dynamite." That is what Christianity is all about, as validated by a long line of faithful witnesses down through the centuries—men and women who have overcome kingdoms, stopped the mouths of lions, quenched the fury of fire, turned aside the edge of the sword. By God's grace they grew strong in battle and put to flight their enemies. By faith they ran through troops and leaped over walls. All these exploits are summed up in the words of the apostle Paul: "I can do all things through Christ which strengtheneth me" (Philippians 4:13).

How we need men and women with that kind of faith today! Are you one of them? Or are you one who has never felt called to accomplish great exploits for God? To attempt great things in his name and to believe him for their completion? This is indeed what he calls us to do. This is what he wishes to give us the power to do, if we will but place our faith in him.

God wants to make the world marvel, to melt frigid indifference and startle people, to make them wide-eyed at what faith can accomplish. When the world saw the boldness of Peter and John, it marveled. Does the world marvel when it looks at you and me? When it sees the boldness that will run through a troop and leap over a wall, it will marvel indeed!

"MADE FOR GREATER THINGS"

DeWitt Talmage, the great preacher of yesteryear, used to tell a story about this Newfoundland dog, Nick. Nick was a handsome beast of great proportion, with a square jaw and a firm gaze that made it clear he would not accept too much meddling from a stranger.

Nick would accompany Dr. Talmage on his daily walks, and all the mongrels and curs in the neighborhood would get stirred up. They would come racing from the doorsteps and out of their kennels, yapping and howling, as Nick and his master walked by. They attacked Nick from all sides, sniping and barking.

Sometimes Dr. Talmage would say to Nick, "Old boy, why do you put up with all this? Why don't you go after them?" But Nick never took his master's advice. He just trotted along serenely, disdainful of the herd yapping behind him.

Dr. Talmage liked to imagine Nick saying, "I am a Newfoundland. I have been created for great things. My father pulled three men out of the surf and saved them from drowning. My uncle on my mother's side dragged a man home who had nearly frozen to death in an avalanche. Should you find some noble enterprise, some great task that needs to be accomplished, just point the way and I shall be glad to undertake it. But as for attending to these spotted curs, I have neither the time nor the inclination. Since it pleases them and does not hurt me, let them yap. I have been made for greater things."

I suspect Nick had more wisdom imputed to him than

many of us have. We spend our time yapping at the little things that nip at our heels, fighting trivial battles, never realizing that we have been made for greater things that could be accomplished through faith in God.

PLUGGING IN

You and I never originate power. We always, and only, receive it.

Is this not true even of our physical strength? Do we not derive it from the food we eat? Take the strongest man and deprive him of food long enough, and he will soon be too weak even to lift his head. Or consider an electrical power station. Does it really create power? Not at all. It simply takes power that already exists in some latent form—either water or oil or the nucleus of the atom—and transforms it into electricity.

Recently I toured a printing plant where I saw a mammoth printing press a story-and-a-half high. Huge rolls of paper were fed into this machine and then cut, printed, turned, folded, stamped, and made into booklets at astonishing speed. This press exuded tremendous power. It was a wonder to behold.

Yet all a person would have to do was reach down and pull the plug, and those great wheels would grind to a halt. The lights would go out, the whirring would stop, and that huge machine would just stand there, powerless.

I think many Christians are like that. God has made us for great things, yet we are unplugged from him. So we stand powerless. We need to "plug in," by faith, into the dynamo of God which is the Holy Spirit. Then the power of God can flow into us and empower us to accomplish great things.

OVERCOMING BY FAITH

Do we not each have our own walls to leap? I do not know what temptations come at you like yapping dogs, trying to overwhelm your spiritual resources and cause you to fall into sin and guilt. I do not know what personal problems you have in your life. I do not know what is happening in your family, what walls of separation and division have been erected. I do not know what challenges you face in your business. But I *do* know that it is possible to run through those troops and to leap over those walls, because God has told us it is so.

How do we do it? By faith! Consider how you entered into eternal life. Did you not come to the place where you rested your hopes on the promise of God, that Christ paid for your salvation and was offering it freely to those who would trust in him? And in the very act of trusting, it was done! In the very act of believing that we have eternal life, we do in fact have it!

Just so, in the very act of believing that we can run through a troop, we become like David, taking up his sword and scattering the host of the Amalekites. We become like David, who with a mighty shout leaps over a wall that had seemed impossible to scale. We believe that God will enable us to do it. And in the believing, it is done.

TAKING ACTION

But notice that there was action on David's part as well. "I *have run*. I *have leaped*." He did not just sit there and tremble in the face of the troop that confronted him. He did not just walk along the wall, feeling it, examining its height. He did not just wait for God to make his problems disappear.

No, David took his sword in his hand and rushed into the fray. Then and only then did his enemies scatter before him. David gathered himself together and rushed at the wall. Then and only then was he able to leap over it.

So it is with us. We must arise and take action. Then we will experience the empowerment of the God who promised us, "Call unto me, and I will answer thee, and shew thee great and mighty things, which thou knowest not" (Jeremiah 33:3). Then we will see the enemy host scatter. Then we will find ourselves being transported over the wall. Then we will see the base metals turned to gold. Then we will give glory to God and cause the unbelieving world to marvel!

TEN

The Triumphs of Faith

For I am persuaded, that neither death, nor life, nor angels, nor principalities, nor powers, nor things present, nor things to come, nor height, nor depth, nor any other creature, shall be able to separate us from the love of God, which is in Christ Jesus our Lord. Romans 8:38-39

EVERYONE WANTS TO BE A WINNER in the game of life. Everyone wants to be a conqueror in the battle of life. Yet, as we look about us, we see many who are not the victors but the vanquished. Many fall short of the hopes they held, their dreams dashed on the cold rocks of reality, leaving them desolate, discouraged, despondent.

What is the secret to victory in life? Many answers have been proposed to this question. Education, some say, is the great panacea, the key that unlocks the door to success. Others say the key is a positive mental attitude: maintain that, and all else will fall into place. Still others point to meditation. Chant your mantra, they advise, and soon life will be mystically transformed into a bowl of cherries. The list goes on and on.

NO LITTLE THING

The Bible also speaks of a key to victory in life. It talks about a key that inevitably leads to triumph: the key of faith. "Faith," the apostle John wrote, "is the victory that overcometh the world" (see 1 John 5:4). With faith, the Bible says, it is *impossible* that we should ultimately fail.

Faith seems like such a little thing. Often, in fact, it seems like nothing at all. I recall the moment when I accepted Christ, when the light of the gospel of grace first brightened my heart and I placed my trust in Christ as Savior and Lord. It was "no big deal." No angelic choirs burst into song, no celestial orchestra broke forth. It was quiet, simple.

I remember thinking to myself, what did my decision amount to? I was a little embarrassed by its ordinariness, and glad that no one asked me about it. I certainly had no inkling of the tremendous repercussions it was to have. What difference did it make, this simple act, after which everything seemed to remain just as it had been before?

Yet the truth was that everything had been dramatically changed: transformed by faith.

Let me be clear that in talking about faith, I am not talking about a vague feeling that "everything is going to work out for the best somehow." I am not talking about "having faith in faith," as some people seem to profess. I mean a conscious decision to place my entire life under the care of a God who loved me enough to die on the cross for me—what theologians call "saving faith." It is this kind of faith that makes us victorious in life.

The eighth chapter of Paul's letter to the Romans speaks of the transforming power of faith, which is one of the crucial ingredients in God's alchemy. I'd like to discuss several "triumphs of faith" that Paul describes in this passage.

FREEDOM FROM GUILT

The first is that *no charge can be brought against those who have faith.* "Who shall lay any thing to the charge of God's elect? It is God that justifieth" (v. 33).

Note especially the words *any thing.* Paul does not limit his claim to some narrow spectrum, but examines life in its entirety, from beginning to end, under the bright light of God's holy law. He arraigns it before the bar of God's perfect justice, before his divine retribution. It is in that light that he makes the sweeping statement, who shall lay *any thing* to the charge of God's elect?

Now, I do not know about you, but it seems that an almost infinite number of things could be laid to *my* charge! Yet as the bowmen line up their arrows of accusation to pierce my heart, God reaches down from heaven and places the cross of Christ between them and me, and all their arrows are stopped.

Paul explains this marvelous, merciful dynamic by saying simply, "It is God that justifieth." This means that those who would lay a charge against me must actually lay it against God. All sin is sin against God, as David pointed out (see Psalm 51:4). Yet God has justified me. He has declared me innocent. He has issued a divine pardon on my behalf.

How different this is from the situation of the unbeliever,

who lives a life tormented by guilt. He knows that a thousand accusations have been made, are being made, and will be made against him. And he knows that in most cases he is guilty as charged! His conscience weighs him down. But for the believer, this crushing, overwhelming burden of guilt has been lifted from his shoulders and placed upon Christ.

THE HANGING JUDGE

Second, Paul says that *no condemnation can come upon those who have faith.* "There is therefore now no condemnation to them which are in Christ Jesus" (v. 1).

Not only can no case be made against us, but even if a case *could* be made, no conviction could ever be obtained! Why? Because Jesus Christ is the judge! "The Father . . . hath committed all judgment unto the Son," Scripture says (John 5:22). It is Christ who will judge the heavens and the earth. It is before his judgment seat that all men shall appear. Jesus Christ, who died to save us, is the one who will judge us.

I once received a letter from a man who was in jail, awaiting trial on some very serious charges. He was filled with apprehension, he said, because he had been told that his case was to be heard by a judge who was known as "the hanging judge." Can you imagine sitting in jail, waiting to go to court, knowing you are guilty, and knowing that you are to be brought before the "hanging judge?"

And yet that is precisely our situation, yours and mine. The one before whom we are to appear at the end, to give an account of our lives, is precisely "the hanging judge"; he is the one who hung upon the cross at Calvary so that we might be delivered from condemnation.

Imagine that you have been accused of a crime. You go to a friend who is a lawyer and ask him to defend you. Since you know him to be an excellent lawyer, you are encouraged by the fact that he agrees to take your case. And yet ... who knows what the judge may do? Anxiously you await his appearance. Finally the bailiff comes out and says, "All rise!" And there, clothed in his black judicial robes, stands the judge—who turns out to be your friend, your lawyer!

So it is in our case. Christ, the one to whom all judgment is given, the judge of heaven and earth, is also our advocate. Even now, Scripture says, Jesus makes intercessions for us before the throne of God (see Hebrews 7:25). There is no condemnation for those who are in Christ Jesus.

Again, how different for the unbeliever. Dread of approaching condemnation pursues him all the days of his life. But for those who have faith in Christ, there is no condemnation.

GROUND FOR REJOICING

The third point is that *no evil can befall those who have faith.* "And we know that all things work together for good to them that love God, to them who are the called according to his purpose" (v. 28).

If there is one thing that robs life of its joy, it is the knowledge that pain and difficulty lie in wait for us, it seems, around every corner. Yet as we have seen, Paul here assures us that any evil that comes our way will be changed into good by the alchemy of God's grace.

Were it not for this truth, it would be impossible for us ever to truly rejoice. Oh, there might be times when everything seemed to go "just right." Business is good . . . your relationship with your spouse is smooth . . . your children are doing well . . . your health is strong . . . your income is secure . . . at times like these you could say, "Today I can rejoice!" But how many days are like that?

Still, the command of Scripture is that we rejoice *always*. How can we rejoice when we are beset on all sides by trials, problems, evils of every sort that threaten to overwhelm us? Only because we have the sure knowledge that they will all be worked together by God for our good. In that assurance we can take our rest.

What a wondrous thing to realize that for the believer, evil is changed into good, whereas for the unbeliever, even good ultimately works for evil. Every blessing he receives only adds to his guilt because of his lack of thankfulness, and his refusal to submit his life to Christ. But what greater triumph could be imagined than to have evil turned to good, through faith in Christ?

THE GREAT GIFT

Fourth, we are told that *no good thing will be withheld from those who have faith.* "He that spared not his own Son, but delivered him up for us all, how shall he not with him also freely give us all things?" (v. 32).

If I were to give you a forty-carat diamond, would I even think of withholding the box in which it came? If I were to give you the life of my only child, is there anything else that I would not freely give?

So it is with God. He has given us his Son, Jesus Christ. How shall he not also give us all things with him? In the one gift, all other gifts are included. We do not deserve such generosity and could never earn it. God gives to us freely, and withholds nothing.

The unbeliever, though some good things in life come his way for a time, knows nothing of the ultimate gift, the gift of eternal life. By rejecting the one great gift, he exempts himself from God's promise to give us all good things as well.

THE CRYSTAL STREAM

Fifth, we are told that *no power can separate those who have faith from the love of God.* "For I am persuaded, that neither death, nor life, nor angels, nor principalities, nor powers, nor things present, nor things to come, nor height, nor depth, nor any other creature, shall be able to separate us from the love of God, which is in Christ Jesus our Lord" (vv. 38-39). What an incredible promise!

Some years ago a crowd of spectators were lined up along the rail watching the magnificent spectacle of Niagara Falls. Millions of tons of water rushed over the cataract and thundered onto the rocks below, creating a great bubbling, boiling foam and mist. What a majestic sight to behold!

Then, suddenly, mysteriously, inexplicably, it all stopped. The great cascade of water simply ceased. The roar died away to an eerie silence. The people stared in amazement. They did not know that somewhere upstream, on that cold winter day, several huge floes of ice had come together to form a dam that, at least for a short time, turned off the falls.

Well, the great cataract of Niagara may be cut off, but the crystal stream that flows from the heart of God in heaven, the stream of his love that has flowed from time immemorial, will continue to flow through all eternity. And nothing can ever stop that pure living water. Nothing can ever separate us from the love of God.

THE GLORY TO BE REVEALED

Finally, we are told that *nothing can compare to the glory that awaits those who have faith.* "For I reckon that the sufferings of this present time are not worthy to be compared with the glory which shall be revealed in us" (v. 18).

I hope that as you endure times of suffering you will remember these words. The difficulties you now experience are insignificant in light of the glory that is to be revealed in you. Can you imagine what that glory might be like when we stand, with renewed bodies and transformed minds, in the midst of men and women made just, as part of the general assembly of the church of the firstborn, triumphant in the paradise of God, forever young, forever healthy, forever rejoicing in our God? Then we will have forgotten these sufferings, as a woman beholding her newborn forgets the travail of giving birth. What a day that will be!

How mighty is this final triumph of faith when we compare it with the situation of the unbeliever, who runs the terrible risk of eternal suffering in the world to come.

John Calvin suffered from a number of serious diseases during his lifetime. In the end he succumbed to asthma. As he lay dying, the leaders of the church of Geneva were gathered around him. Calvin encouraged them in how they were to carry on after he was gone. Then, gasping for breath, he uttered his last words: "For I reckon that the sufferings of this present world are not worthy to be compared with..." He never said it; but he experienced it: "... the glory which is to be revealed in us."

These are the triumphs of faith. Though it may seem that nothing changed when you placed your trust in Christ, the truth is that everything has changed. God has made all things new. Truly this is the victory that overcomes the world: our faith!

ELEVEN

The Sin of Aiming Low

And after him was Shamgar the son of Anath, which slew of the Philistines six hundred men with an ox goad: and he also delivered Israel. **Judges 3:31**

T O FALL IS NO CRIME. But to aim low is! Such has been the opinion of all the people who have greatly influenced this world. Is it yours?

It was certainly the opinion of Shamgar. Now, perhaps you are not intimately acquainted with Shamgar. But you should be. He was a remarkable man in many ways.

Other than one verse that describes something of the times in which he lived, there is but a single verse in the whole Bible that speaks of Shamgar. But those few words tell us a great deal. It is the verse that is written at the top of this page. Let's take a brief look at the historical setting so we can appreciate the full significance of this verse.

The Philistines were a neighboring people who had conquered the Israelites, their perennial thorn in the flesh. Now that they had triumphed over them, they were oppressing them sorely and systematically. First, they had collected all the swords and weapons of war and taken them out of Israel. Then, to make sure Israel could not rise from its state of subjugation, the Philistines deported all their blacksmiths. Not only did they have no weapons, but they now had no way to make new ones!

Needless to say, the Israelites were despondent. They had lost faith in themselves. They had even lost faith in their God. Their situation seemed hopeless. The Philistines were so numerous, so powerful, so well-armed. What could the Israelites do?

SEEING PAST THE PROBLEM

But there was one man who could see past the problem to the opportunity. His name was Shamgar. He was not a general, nor an admiral, not even a sergeant or a private. In fact, so far as we know, he was not even in the army. This man may never have had any military training whatsoever. He was a farmer. That was his only claim to fame.

What Shamgar could do was to break a yoke of oxen and use them to till the soil. That may not sound like much to you and me. But in fact it was an act of tremendous courage, even of defiance. Typically, after seeds had been planted in Israel, after many days had passed and much hard work had been done, when the fields were nearly ready for harvest—then the Philistines would sweep down and carry away the crops. All the farmer's hard work would go for naught. We read in the Bible that roads were grown over and villages left empty because the people of Israel were in hiding from the dreaded Philistine conquerors.

But Shamgar was not content to let it be that way. He went out, plowed his field with his ox, and planted his crops. Sure enough, as harvest time approached so did the Philistines. More than six hundred of them swept down on this one, poor, isolated farmer, who had nothing with which to defend himself but an ox goad.

NO EXCUSES

An ox goad was simply a length of wood, often made from a limb of an oak tree. It would typically be eight to ten feet in length. The bark would be stripped away and a sharp iron point affixed to one end. It was used, as its name suggests, to jab at an ox, goading it to move along when it balked. To the other end was attached a flattened piece of metal, used to scrape off the dirt that accumulated on the blade of the plow.

Not a very sophisticated weapon of war! But in the hands of a strong man who knew how to wield it, the ox goad could be quite lethal indeed. And so it was in the hands of Shamgar. When those six hundred Philistines descended upon him, Shamgar decided he had had enough.

It certainly would have been easy enough for Shamgar to do nothing. Think of the many excuses that were readily at hand. *They are soldiers, and I am just a farmer. I don't even have a sword. There is really nothing I can do. I have to just let them come in and do as they wish.*

But that is not what Shamgar said! Because of the faith he had in God ... because of the concern he had for his people

. . . because of his own dignity as a human being . . . he decided to take a stand, come what may. As the Philistines swooped down, Shamgar took that ox goad and began to swing.

There must have been some astonished Philistines that day! Eight feet of solid oak, with iron implements at each end, in the hands of a sturdy, enraged, faith-filled servant of God—the Philistines must have thought they had wandered into a hive of angry bees. They were getting it from all sides, being jabbed and cut and pounded. And when the dust had settled, the six hundred Philistines lay dead on the ground, and Shamgar went back to his harvest. The Bible notes with eloquent simplicity: "and he also delivered Israel."

THE IMPORTANCE OF AIMING HIGH

I believe we can learn some important lessons from this simple farmer who accomplished so much in his day. Most of all, we can learn about the evil of aiming low. Most Christians—and most other people as well—never accomplish much, because they never set out to accomplish much. They are satisfied with low ambition, or no ambition at all. And when you aim at nothing, you're sure to hit it!

Have you ever written down goals for your life? I mean spiritual goals, things that you believe the Lord wants you to accomplish for his sake and for the sake of his kingdom. All those who write on the subject of attaining success, in any realm, point to the importance of spelling out clear, precise goals. Such goals will help to motivate us to great accomplishments.

I would like to suggest five things that I think will be important if your life is to be counted a success when you stand before your Maker. Unless we have done these five things, our lives will not have been as successful as they could have been—as successful as God wanted them to be.

GODLY GOALS

First, we need to set godly goals. Many people in this world set goals. Many of those goals, from a human perspective, seem like noble ones. But from God's perspective these people have never lifted their vision out of the mud. They are still groveling in the dirt of earthly achievement. They have set goals, all right, but not godly ones. We can never get away from the truth expressed in the familiar couplet:

Only one life, 'twill soon be past
Only what's done for Christ will last.

What will it be for you and for me? Wood, hay, and stubble? Or gold, silver, and precious stones? How many lives will be built only of the former! How much happier will those be whose lives have been built to stand forever! "Seek ye first the kingdom of God, and his righteousness," Jesus said, "and all these things shall be added unto you" (Matthew 6:33).

What have you accomplished for the kingdom of God? What do you aim to accomplish? Have you accomplished anything tangible, anything you can really put your finger on? How many people are now walking with the Lord because of you? We need to set not only long-range, lifelong goals, but also short-term goals that help us see whether or not we are really progressing in the right direction.

BURNING DESIRE

Second, we must set our hearts on reaching our goals. The Bible says, "Set your affection on things above" (Colossians 3:2). This refers to a conscious, deliberate focusing of our will and desire on what we wish to see come about.

Christians are often good at intellectualizing about what they would like to see happen for the kingdom. Many are good at analyzing what it will take to make it happen. Some are good at sermonizing about how important the kingdom is and how worthwhile their goals are. But when you get right down to it, those kingdom goals are not where their hearts are. The fact is that they have another set of goals, unnamed and undefined but no less real, that command their affections and, therefore, control their lives.

I frequently urge people in my congregation to bring others to church with them on Sundays. I know, and they know, that this is one of the simplest and most effective ways to help other men and women make contact with the Lord. *Bring people to church*—who could argue with that? Who would deny that it is a worthy and godly goal? Yet isn't it astonishing how few people actually follow through on it? We all acknowledge that it is a good goal, but we don't do it. Our *true* goals are elsewhere.

I like to tell the story of one lady who *did* decide to take this goal to heart. One week she invited not one, not two, not three, but *fifty-two people* to church. And they all came! If every Christian worked that hard to build the kingdom, what a different world this would be!

Rudyard Kipling once said something in this regard that I think is very incisive. If we have goals in life but have not attained them, Kipling said, it shows either that we did not *really* want them, or that we decided not to pay the price. Isn't that often the case? May God grant us the burning desire to see the glory of Jesus Christ cover the earth, to see men and women brought out of darkness into light, out of bondage into freedom. May it become the consuming passion of each and every one of us!

GREAT EXPECTATIONS

Third, we must expect great things from God. The psalmist wrote, "My soul, wait thou only upon God; for my expectation is from him" (Psalm 62:5). Is your expectation from yourself? From your education, your intelligence, your wisdom? Is it from money or power or influence? Our expectation must be from God! Having set godly goals, we must look to him to bring them to fruition.

One of the tragedies of life is that so many people live their whole lives without ever finding out what they were here for. If only they had known what they were supposed to do, perhaps they might have done it. Instead they wander, just as the Israelites wandered in the wilderness for forty years. They wander through life for thirty years, or sixty, or eighty, never really knowing where they are going. They are like a baseball player roaming center field inning after inning, watching fly balls soar over his head and ground balls race past his feet, never understanding until after the final out what the game was all about.

That is the way it is with many Christians. They do not know what the game is about. It is not about *our* goals, *our* talents, *our* efforts, *our* achievements. It is about letting God accomplish his will through us. We need to learn to expect great things from God!

THE MENACE OF MEDIOCRITY

Fourth, we must prepare ourselves. There are many people whom God would like to use but cannot, because they are not prepared. How much time we fritter away! How little knowledge of the Scripture we have, how little time we devote to studying it in preparation for being used by God. The Word of God is referred to as "the sword of the Spirit" (Ephesians 6:17). Unless we can effectively use God's Word, we cannot be effectively used *by* God, since his Word is his weapon.

I once heard of a pastor who preached a sermon on "The Menace of Mediocrity." He was talking about people in his church who never seemed to do anything for God. "If an automobile had as many useless parts as the church has useless members, it wouldn't even roll down a hill," he lamented.

These are strong words, but no stronger than the Bible uses itself. James speaks of the importance of being active in God's service:

> What doth it profit, my brethren, though a man say he hath faith, and have not works? Can faith save him? If a brother or sister be naked, and destitute of daily food, and one of you say unto them, Depart in peace, be ye warmed and filled; notwithstanding ye give them not those things which are needful to the body; what doth it profit? Even so faith, if it hath not works, is dead. . . .
>
> James 2:14-17

Even so, I am confident that if anyone with a sincere desire to be used will prepare himself—will "study to show thyself approved, a workman that needeth not to be ashamed" (2 Timothy 2:15)—God *will* use him and glorify himself through him.

DON'T JUST SIT THERE

Finally, we must attempt great things for God. By this I mean that we must not only *dream* of great things, and *desire* great things, and *expect* great things, and *prepare* for great things— we must actually get up out of our chairs and set about *doing* them.

Imagine a military man who spent his whole career at West Point but never went to war: he knows everything there is to know about battles, but he has never actually fought one. Or imagine a woman who makes a lifelong study of skydiving: she knows how to pack and unpack a parachute, she has perfected her landing, she knows all the mysteries of air currents, but she has never actually jumped out of an airplane. Would you not say there was something incomplete about such people?

Again, James takes to task those who pursue their Christianity in this fashion:

> But be ye doers of the word, and not hearers only, deceiving your own selves. For if any be a hearer of the word, and not a doer, he is like unto a man beholding his natural face in a glass: For he beholdeth himself, and goeth his way, and straightway forgetteth what manner of man he was.
>
> But whoso looketh into the perfect law of liberty, and continueth therein, he being not a forgetful hearer, but a doer of the work, this man shall be blessed in his deed. James 1:22-25

We are blessed, James says, in the *doing* of God's will, not merely in the pondering of it. God is ready and willing— even eager—to turn our trials into triumphs, our base metal into gold. And do it he will—as we join our wills to his and *take action* in pursuit of the goals he sets before us.

OVERCOMING THE OBSTACLE COMPLEX

Psychologists tell us we suffer from numerous complexes in America today. Surely one of the most common must be the "obstacle complex." You know the symptoms: "Oh, that would never work! I could never do that. It's never been done before. I don't have what it takes. There aren't enough of us. The enemy is too big. The difficulties are too great. I'm just one person. What could I do?" That is how people sound who suffer from the "obstacle complex." Are you one of them?

Shamgar wasn't. He had a goal: to free his people from bondage. Now I suppose virtually every Israelite had that same goal somewhere in his mind. But Shamgar didn't leave it there. He set his affections on it until it became a burning passion in his heart. In spite of the obstacles, he prepared himself, trusting that God would somehow bring it to pass.

And then, when the time came, Shamgar took action. He didn't stand around all his life wishing it would happen. He decided he was going to do it, and he was going to do it *now.* And he did! Shamgar was just a lowly farmer, but "he also delivered Israel" (Judges 3:31). This unsung man with nothing but an oaken ox goad to his name became the leader of the entire nation. Why? Because he attempted a great thing for God, and by the grace of God, he did it.

Failure, indeed, is no crime. But aiming low *is.* Let's make it a crime we'll never be found guilty of!

TWELVE

When Tempted to Quit

And let us not be weary in welldoing: for in due season we shall reap, if we faint not. Galatians 6:9

IN THE ANCIENT GREEK MYTH, Orpheus loses his beautiful wife Eurydice and, with lyre in hand, makes his way through the darkness of the underworld in search of her.

At last Orpheus reaches Pluto, the god of the nether world. He agrees to allow Orpheus to take his wife Eurydice back, on one condition: that he not set his eyes on her until they reach the land of light above.

And so they set off—Orpheus in the lead, beautiful Eurydice following. They pass one obstacle and danger after another. All hell holds its breath as they make their tortuous way upward. Finally Orpheus catches his first glimpse of light. They are almost home! So elated is Orpheus that he turns to tell his wife the good news—and in that moment, all his labor is lost and Eurydice vanishes.

SECRETS OF SUCCESS

This ancient myth dramatically teaches a great truth: only the one who perseveres to the end will be saved. How we start is not the only thing that matters; how we finish counts, too.

In the twelfth chapter of Genesis we find a verse which, despite its rather homely language, conveys a great truth. In fact it conveys two secrets of success that apply to any sphere of life. Yet most people miss them altogether.

> And Abram took Sarai his wife, and Lot his brother's son, and all their substance that they had gathered, and the souls that they had gotten in Haran; and they went forth to go into the land of Canaan; and into the land of Canaan they came. **Genesis 12:5**

Do you see in this verse the two great secrets of success in life? The first is simply this: We must select a noble goal, a goal worthy of our efforts. The second is that we must *keep going*. It is not enough merely to begin. We must "keep on keepin' on."

Simple, isn't it? The beginning, the end, and the necessity of perseverance in between. *They set forth to go into the land of Canaan, and into the land of Canaan they came.*

TEMPTED TO QUIT

How many people have set out on journeys in life but not seen them through to the end? They begin well, but something happens and they fall by the wayside. "Many of his disciples went back, and walked no more with him," we read (John 6:66). How different they were from the apostle Paul, who in his last epistle writes, "I have finished my course" (2 Timothy 4:7).

The temptation to quit is ever-present. I am sure all of us have faced it. I suspect, in fact, that the temptation to quit is far more prevalent than most of us think, and that we have all succumbed to it more often than we even dream.

There is, first of all, the temptation to quit following after Christ, to turn aside from the path of discipleship. The devil continually says to us, in an infinite variety of ways, "You've blown it. There is no profit in following Christ. Seek the good things of the world and pursue them instead." And many do precisely that.

There is the temptation to quit our job. It may not be the case that we are each called to do some particular job all our lives. But I believe that many people never succeed in their occupations because they flit from one thing to another like a butterfly hopping from one flower to another. They don't stick with any one thing long enough to succeed at it.

Many are tempted to quit their marriages. How many have given in to this temptation, instead of seeking God's help and working out difficulties by his grace?

WHEN THE GOING GETS TOUGH

There are many reasons why we quit, some no doubt better than others. They may seem eminently reasonable at the time. But in the final analysis, the reason why we quit will not count for anything. The fact will remain: we quit!

How many of us set out to be faithful witnesses to our

Lord, determined that we would testify to him at every opportunity? And we quit! Well, we say, the going got tough. Yes, but as the old saying goes, when the going gets tough, the tough get going. In the same situation, the weak quit.

How many of us committed ourselves to be faithful stewards of the blessings the Lord gave us? We were going to tithe and give our alms and offerings. But we quit, and so the blessings God promises to faithful stewards have not come to us.

How many of us set out to develop some talent that God gave us? We were going to learn to sing, or to play an instrument, or to paint. But the books and materials we bought are still taking up space on a shelf somewhere. We quit!

How many of us have faced the difficulties of daily life and simply given up? How many people have quit on life altogether, have abandoned their posts, have rushed impetuously into the next life? Suicide is the ultimate form of quitting.

GOING WITH THE FLOW

Some of us have given in to these temptations so often, we have forgotten that we ever quit in the first place. We have lived in Quittersville so long we cannot remember any other way of life. We surrendered to the enemy so many years ago we don't even remember that we are now a prisoner of war. We have settled for a lower aim. We had higher aspirations once, but now we are content simply to get through the day.

The temptation to quit is very subtle, different from every other temptation. Every other temptation tries to lure us into something that will require some effort. But it takes no effort to quit. If you wanted to rob a bank, you would have a great deal of hard work ahead of you. How many people would be bank robbers except that they are too lazy? I am sure there are people who would become adulterers except for the fact that adultery takes so much work.

Most sin requires that we *do* something. But to quit, we don't do anything! We just stop. Sit down. Fold our hands. Give up.

The temptation to quit is a temptation to stop our battle against entropy, that principle of life by which everything tends toward disorder and chaos. We try to build things up, but they seem to be forever taking themselves apart. So we lie back and quit. "Go with the flow," we say. But what we do not realize is that "the flow" is going down the drain! Even a dead fish can float downstream. But it takes a great deal of effort to swim against the tide of a corrupt world.

ON PROBATION

There is a crucial significance to the temptation to quit which we often miss because we do not understand the nature of life. If you would ask a hundred people to finish the sentence, "Life is . . ." you would likely get a hundred different answers. But the answer given by the Bible is very simple: it tells us that life is a time of probation.

Many modern people do not grasp this, because they do not understand that there is a God to whom we must each give an account of every minute, every hour, every ounce of energy, every talent, every penny we have had at our disposal. We have been called by God to a divine purpose in life, and we are equipped by him to pursue and attain it with his help. Thus our success in life depends on not quitting.

Of course, the secular vocabulary is filled with phrases and expressions that warn us not to give up, give in, cave in, pass out, fall down, keel over, sink under, throw in the towel, cash in our chips, go over the hill, give up the ghost, hang up our spikes, or jump ship. Instead we are urged to hang in there, to stick with it, to tough it out, to see it through, to come out fighting. But without a clear understanding of life as a time of probation, we find it all too easy to give in to the temptation to quit.

THE ANCHOR OF HOPE

How does Satan bring this temptation upon us? Most of the time, he tempts us to quit through the all-too-familiar voice of discouragement. We have all heard its whisperings: "You can't do it. You'll never make it. You don't have what it takes. You might as well pack it in right now."

Sound familiar? Have you heard this litany of despair? Of course you have. We all have. It makes no difference how high or low we may be on the social scale, how much or how little success we might have attained thus far. The temptation to quit visits us all.

What is the answer? How are we going to resist this temptation that threatens to short-circuit the divine alchemy by which God turns all things, even our trials, to gold?

The great missionary, William Carey, said that no enterprise can ever be carried out without hope of success. The Bible says, "Now abideth faith, hope, charity, these three" (1 Corinthians 13:13). Faith looks to the past and builds on what God has done. Hope looks to the future and anchors itself in what God has *promised* to do.

Trusting in the promises of God and having hope for a victorious future enable us to live a life of love in the present. Hope is a powerful motivator. We need to take God at his word when he guarantees that we can do all things through him who strengthens us (see Philippians 4:13), and let that assurance give us hope.

A CLOUD OF WITNESSES

We can also be encouraged not to quit by the example of the "cloud of witnesses" (see Hebrews 12:1) who have persevered and seen ultimate victory. We can look at Abraham who obeyed God and reached the land of Canaan. We can look at the apostle Paul, who at the end of a long and tumultuous life could say, "I have fought a good fight, I have finished my course, I have kept the faith: henceforth there is laid up for me a crown of righteousness" (2 Timothy 4:7-8).

When you think of Abraham Lincoln, what qualities come to mind? Compassion? Concern for the common man? Justice? Humor? I think that if we really knew Lincoln, we would see that the overriding quality of his character was nothing other than perseverance.

Abraham Lincoln may have been one of the most successful failures who over lived. Consider his final resume:

1831—Failed in business
1832—Defeated for legislature
1833—Again failed in business
1835—Sweetheart died
1836—Suffered nervous breakdown
1838—Defeated for Speaker
1840—Defeated for Elector
1843—Defeated for Congress
1848—Again defeated for Congress
1855—Defeated for Senate
1856—Defeated for Vice-President
1858—Again defeated for Senate
1860—*Elected President of the United States*

When we consider the record of a man who failed so many times before finally achieving such wonderful success, are we not ashamed of the number of times we have given up? A quitter is a loser. Lincoln was never a loser because he never quit. Who among us can even dream of what God could do in and through us if we would yield ourselves wholly to him and never quit?

WHEN TO QUIT

There is, however, one thing that I *do* want to urge you to quit. If you are like most modern men and women, you are trying to earn your way into heaven. Is that the case with you? Are you trying to be "good enough" to please God? To make yourself worthy of paradise? To try, by virtue of your morality, your piety, your benevolence, to secure your right to enter through those gates of pearl?

If so, then I urge you to quit. That's right: quit. You can never succeed. It is *impossible* to earn eternal life by our own efforts. We have God's Word on it: it is "not by works of righteousness which we have done, but according to his mercy he saved us" (Titus 3:5).

Heaven is a free gift. Only Christ was good enough, worthy of paradise. Only he was capable of earning his way into heaven. And he did—not only for himself, but for all of us. When we place our lives under his lordship, we inherit heaven as God's free gift.

POWER TO PERSEVERE

Moreover, when we receive Christ into our hearts, we receive the power of God. We are connected with the divine dynamo of the universe. The Holy Spirit of God comes into us to strengthen us, so that we can indeed "do all things through Christ who strengthens us."

Until Christ comes into our lives, none of the promises of God pertain to us. But when we embrace Jesus, we claim his promises as well. Then the promise of victory is ours!

Are you tempted to quit? Don't! Have you already given up? Then start over! Begin by surrendering to Christ and tapping into the power of the Holy Spirit. He will enable you to "keep on keepin' on," to persevere until you attain to the noble goal he has given you in life!

THIRTEEN

Pressing Toward the Mark

... This one thing I do, forgetting those things which are behind, and reaching forth unto those things which are before, I press toward the mark for the prize of the high calling of God in Christ Jesus. Philippians 3:13-14

WHY IS IT THAT SOME PEOPLE SUCCEED in life while others fail? Is it heredity? Luck? Circumstances? Money? Education? I suppose all these contribute in some cases. Yet don't we all know people who have enjoyed all these advantages and still amounted to very little? And history is replete with examples of individuals who had none of these advantages, yet succeeded magnificently.

What *are* the secrets of success? I believe the Bible, especially through the writings of the apostle Paul, tells us. In just one simple verse from his letter to the Philippians, Paul gives us four secrets of success. I go so far as to call them *laws* of success, because I am certain that anyone who ignores or violates them cannot ultimately succeed, no matter how many other advantages he or she may enjoy. They are principles through which God works in turning to gold the challenges and struggles we face.

"THIS ONE THING"

First of all, Paul says, *"This one thing I do."* He makes it clear that he has a definite purpose in life. *The first great law of success is to constantly have before your mind the goal toward which you are headed.*

The importance of having a clearly defined goal cannot be overestimated. Someone has said that a journey of a thousand miles begins with a single step. I am convinced that most people who fail are doomed from the first step they take, because they don't clearly know their destination.

Can you say, "This one thing I do?" And can you articulate clearly what that "one thing" is? The problem for most of us is that we jump on our horse and ride off in ten different directions at once.

It is not surprising that we are so confused. We receive all kinds of confusing signals about what our goal in life *should* be. The evolutionists will tell us that there *is* no such thing as purpose. If the cosmos appears to be moving in any particular direction, they say, that is just appearance. According to their view of reality, all things are simply the result of random change. Is it any wonder that people who spend the first twenty years of their lives being taught this philosophy have little sense of direction?

Then there are the psychologists who tell us just the opposite: that there is a purpose behind *everything* we do.

Of course, in their estimation, most of these purposes are beyond our control. They lie hidden, stashed away somewhere in the basement of our psyche, influencing us subconsciously.

THE SPIRITUAL JUNK HEAP

The Bible sends no such contradictory signals. It makes abundantly clear that God has given a grand purpose to all things. Events are not just spinning randomly across the stage of time. They are moving toward a definite conclusion, when everything will reach its ordained goal and God will lower the curtain on human history.

This is true for the cosmos, as well as each and every individual. All of us have been given a divinely ordained purpose that we are to fulfill in our lives. The Bible makes it plain that if we fail to fulfill the purpose God has given us, our lives will end in tragic failure.

Years ago my wife and I bought a marvelous little gadget: an electric can opener. It was a wonder to behold—color-coordinated with our wallpaper, with shiny chrome adding a touch of brightness to the counter top. It made the cans of corn and peas and dog food turn around and around, with a delightful little *whir*. This electric can opener *sounded* so efficient and busy and helpful. The only problem was that it didn't work. We could never get it to open a single can. Guess where this marvelous little gadget ended up? That's right: on the junk heap.

Outside of ancient Jerusalem was a place called the Valley of Hinnom. We know it better as "Gehenna," which the English version of the Bible translates as "hell." Into

Gehenna was cast all the refuse of the city, the things that had ceased to serve their purpose. That is where people go when they fail to fulfill the purposes God has for them.

SINGULARITY OF PURPOSE

Paul makes clear not only that he had a purpose, but that he had a *single* purpose. "This *one thing* I do." What a difference this makes! *The integration of personality, of all the resources and faculties of our life, into a single purpose is the second great secret of success.*

The handle of an axe has just one purpose: to transfer the force and momentum generated by the woodsman into the head of the axe, and finally into the sharp, knife-like blade as it crashes into a length of timber. When a bowman shoots an arrow, everything—the shaft, the feathers, the bow, the string, the arm and eye of the archer—are mobilized toward one purpose: to drive the head of the arrow into the heart of the target.

Can you imagine a football team that has not integrated its efforts toward the execution of a single play? It sometimes happens that one or two players leave the huddle with the wrong play in mind. The quarterback ends up trying to hand the ball to a running back who thought he was supposed to be blocking for a forward pass. The best that team can hope for in a busted play is to limit the loss of yardage.

Singleness of purpose is a characteristic of every great life. People like the apostle Paul, or David Livingstone, or Florence Nightingale, or Martin Luther, or John Calvin—all were marked by their dedication to marshaling all their energy and talent in the pursuit of a single, overriding objective.

THE *RIGHT* PURPOSE

But wait. Mere singleness of purpose, important as it is, is not enough. We can have a singular purpose and still be a failure in life. Why? Because it is not enough to have merely a *single* purpose. We must also have the *right* purpose. Paul wrote, "*This* one thing I do: I press on toward the high calling of God."

Paul had taken a long look at life and had concluded that it was worth living for one purpose and one purpose only: to follow the call of God. He was to love God with all his heart, mind, soul, and strength. He was to serve him with all his talent and energy. He was to give himself over totally to God's purposes in the world.

So it must be with us. If we have not determined that our business, our recreation, our study, our minds and hearts, our time and money—everything at our disposal—are to be given over to the high call of God, then we will not succeed in life. Indeed, we *cannot.* For the pursuit of God is the only goal which promises success. This is the third secret of success.

GO FOR THE GUSTO?

Ultimately, people choose one of two courses in life. We choose either "the narrow way, which leads to life," or "the broad way, which leads to destruction" (see Matthew 7:13-

14). The narrow way is the path of surrender to God and his purposes. The broad way is the path of egoism, in which we ask, What's in it for me? What am I going to get out of it? How am I going to prosper?

As Jesus observed, most of us choose the broad way. We take the short-term view of life. We conclude that we only go around once in life, and so we must grab all the gusto we can get.

But what if we are wrong? What if God has created us in such a way that we will go around for ever and ever? If all we have done is to grab for the gusto in this life, we will wake up one day to find ourselves in a world of endless heartache and terror.

A young man graduating from college went to say goodbye to his favorite professor. The professor asked about his plans. The young man replied that he had accepted a position as a junior partner in a law firm and hoped one day to become a full partner.

"That's fine," said the professor. "Then what?"

The young man replied, "Actually, in the back of my mind, I've thought about someday entering public service. Perhaps running for office."

"Splendid," said the professor. "And then what?"

"Well," the young man said, "then I suppose I'll retire. Move to Florida. Play some golf."

"I see," the professor nodded. "And then?"

"And then ... " the young man mused. "Well, I suppose then I'll die."

"That is absolutely correct," the professor said. "And then what?"

The young man stood silent for several moments. "I

don't know," he said at last. "I guess I've never thought about that."

The professor shook his head slowly and said, "Young man, you are intelligent, talented, and educated. But you are a fool. Go home and think your life through again."

We must take the long-term view if we are to choose the right path in life.

FORGETTING OUR FAILURES

Paul goes on to say that in pressing toward his goal, he "forgets those things which are behind." This is an amazing statement when we consider how often Scripture tells us to remember. "Remember now thy Creator in the days of thy youth" (Ecclesiastes 12:1). "Remember his marvellous works" (Psalm 105:5). "Remember . . . the commandments of the LORD" (Numbers 15:39).

All these admonitions to remember, and now Paul tells us to forget! *The fourth secret to success in life is knowing what things to remember and what things to forget.* Many people fail in life because they forget what they ought to remember, and cling to what they ought to leave behind.

We ought to forget those things that debilitate us, that keep us from reaching our full potential in Christ. First among these is our failures. I believe that the remembrance of our failures is a chain Satan uses to bind us to the ground like a flightless bird. No matter how determinedly we spread our wings and try to take off, that chain jerks us back to earth.

"I tried it before, and I failed."

"I got up to speak once and forgot what I was going to say."

"I can still remember them laughing at me."

"I didn't do well in school."

"My business went bankrupt."

"I can't do it. I just *know* I can't."

How many people stop themselves from ever succeeding because they will not let themselves forget their past failures?

FORGETTING OUR SUCCESSES

Sometimes we also need to forget our successes. Some of us are accomplished laurel-sitters—resting on our laurels for years. We reach a certain level of attainment and are satisfied with it. That is not what Paul did. He put even his triumphs behind him, and went on to still greater things.

Once Napoleon listened to one of his generals describe a battle he had won: how he had brought the artillery in at just the right time; how his lead force had smashed the center of the enemy line while his reserves crept around and attacked from the rear, assuring a stunning victory. After concluding his narrative, the general waited for Napoleon to pat him on the back. "Yes, yes, very good," Napoleon snapped. "And what did you do the *next* day?"

We may indeed have already registered some praiseworthy accomplishments for the Lord. But what are we doing *now* for the Lord? What will we be doing tomorrow? God grant us a holy discontent that will enable us to forget our successes and press on to new attainments.

PRESSING ON

Finally, Paul speaks of "pressing toward the mark." This speaks not only of eagerness of spirit, but also of the expenditure of effort. The Greek word here translated "to press" means to pursue something aggressively, intensely, almost vehemently. We call upon the Lord to give us the drive, the desire, to accomplish great things for him, and when he does we throw ourselves unreservedly into the tasks he sets before us.

I am not speaking here of the way we attain our salvation. As we have already discussed, eternal life comes to us as a free gift when we place our trust in Christ. Rather, I speak of the way we are to live our lives as human beings who have been redeemed in the blood of Christ and called into the service of the Master of the Universe. God has given us brains and brawn, heart and soul, emotion and will. He has given them to us to be used in the service of his kingdom.

May God give us the grace to clearly understand what our goal in life is, and then, having put behind us everything that would slow us down or hold us back, to press toward it with all the vigor he so mightily inspires within us!

FOURTEEN

Perseverance

But he that shall endure unto the end, the same shall be saved. Matthew 24:13

A MAN ONCE TOLD ME he was "too busy" for religion. Presumably he meant that the demands of seeking success and fulfillment in the secular realm were so great that he could make no time for what he saw as a nice, but not necessary, extracurricular activity.

What he did not realize—what many people do not realize—is that the same qualities that make for success in the spiritual realm also make for success in every other realm of life.

If you question whether that is true, I invite you to peruse any of the hundreds of self-help books that fill the shelves of bookstores everywhere. While they generally evidence a fairly weak grasp of spiritual truth, virtually all their advice is but a restatement of wisdom that is presented—more clearly and more reliably—in the Bible. Some of the authors actually quote the Bible. Others, perhaps without even realizing it, merely echo biblical themes. But my point holds in either case: the teachings of the Bible can make a person's life successful in every sphere.

COMMANDED TO PERSEVERE

Perhaps in no instance is this more true than with the quality of perseverance. Certainly Jesus' statement in Matthew 24 makes clear its vital importance in the spiritual realm: "He that shall endure unto the end, the same shall be saved." No doubt the converse is also true: without perseverance we shall not see the inside of paradise.

He made the same point in the parable of the sower. Some of the good seed, the parable says, fell on rocky ground. The seed sprang up and flourished at first, but in time it fell away. Clearly Jesus was speaking of the spiritual state of those who do not persevere in cultivating the grace of God in their lives.

Of course we Christians rejoice in the greater truth that Scripture also teaches, that "he which hath begun a good work in you will perform it until the day of Jesus Christ" (Philippians 1:6). That is, it is God who is bringing about the "good work" of our salvation, and it is he who will see it through.

Nevertheless, we are commanded to persevere. The account of the passion and death of our Lord, which we hear every year at Easter time, makes this clear. The crucifixion contrasts the example of Judas, the world's greatest quitter, with that of Jesus.

Judas gave up. He gave up on God. He gave up on Jesus, his rabbi. Ultimately he even gave up on himself, committing suicide. But Jesus, as he hung upon the cross, was able to say, "It is finished" (John 19:30). I have completed the work the Father gave me to do. I have seen it through to the end. I have persevered.

Years later the apostle Paul was able to write,

I have fought a good fight, I have finished my course, I have kept the faith: henceforth there is laid up for me a crown of righteousness, which the Lord, the righteous judge, shall give me at that day.... 2 Timothy 4:7-8

Clearly the Bible promises a glorious reward to those who will persevere until the end!

THE BASE AND THE BEAUTIFUL

Scripture seems to treat life as a proving ground, one that is constantly weeding out the quitters in every phase of life. We have already considered the passage that says, "Let us not be weary in welldoing: for in due season we shall reap, if we faint not" (Galatians 6:9).

Now at first this warning seems most unfair. Surely everyone who engages in "welldoing" will find himself weary at one time or another. Indeed, I sometimes think well-doers are the most weary of all the men and women on the face of the earth.

Perhaps we have not adequately grasped the full meaning of this verse. In the original Greek it represents something of a play on words. The word translated "weary" is *kakos*, meaning "ugly" or "base." From it we derive our English word "cacophony," which refers to an ugly, unpleasant noise. The Greek word translated "well-doing" is *kalos*, meaning "beautiful." From it we derive the word "calligraphy," which refers to beautiful writing.

Thus the verse is actually telling us, "Let us not be base in doing beautiful things," referring to the baseness, the ugliness, of giving up.

INSPIRATION AND PERSPIRATION

I think it can safely be said that most successful people owe more to perseverance and persistence than to any other factor. There are those few people who win the state lottery or come into large inheritances. But what kind of success is that? Where is the gratification of seeing your own thoughts, dreams, and efforts come to fruition?

Genius has been described as ten percent inspiration and ninety percent perspiration. We don't like to think of it that way, though. We are quick to credit people's success to "natural talent" or "innate ability"—rather than simply to "hard work."

For example, consider Charles Spurgeon, "prince of pulpiteers," who preached in England a century ago. I have read innumerable comments on Spurgeon's sermons that rhapsodize about his native talent for public speaking. No doubt he did possess a high degree of talent. Yet it is also true that Spurgeon worked hard at enhancing that talent. He studied the art of preaching as few have ever done and learned about the workings of the human voice. As you examine his sermons you cannot help but be impressed by the breadth and depth of his understanding of the subjects he dealt with. Gifted? Certainly. But a great deal of persistent effort went into perfecting those gifts.

DAY AFTER DAY

Or consider the great Greek orator, Demosthenes. He started life as a terribly handicapped stammerer. His affliction even cost him his entire inheritance: because he was unable to stand up in public and defend his rights, what should rightfully have been his was given to someone else. So he set about overcoming his problem. Demosthenes went to the beach and placed pebbles in his mouth to force himself to enunciate clearly. He would practice speaking over the roar of the waves. Day after day, week after week, month after month, this great orator practiced until the name Demosthenes became synonymous with eloquence. What perseverance!

Consider the pyramids, or the other wonders of the ancient world: the canals connecting rivers and oceans, the tunnels piercing the hearts of mountains—all of them done centuries before the machine age. Spend one half-hour swinging a pick or wielding a shovel and you will begin to appreciate the arduous effort and the incredible perseverance it took to produce such amazing results.

ENEMIES OF PERSEVERANCE

Why do so few of us reach the heights of accomplishment of which we are capable? Is it lack of talent? Perhaps, though I doubt this is as large an obstacle as we tend to think. Certainly it is not lack of divine help: God always stands ready to give us what we need, to turn our trials into triumphs, as we apply ourselves in his service. So what is the problem? Ninety-nine times out of a hundred, the difficulty is lack of perseverance. We do not persist. We do not see it through. We do not "endure to the end."

Why not? What are the enemies of perseverance, and how can we defeat them?

First, if we are to persevere, *we must not be deterred by lack of immediate results.* Many of us try once, or twice, or even three times, and then give up if we do not see the results we seek. What if success was waiting for us on the fourth try? Or the tenth? Or the one-hundredth?

I cannot help but think of Thomas Edison in this regard. In making the first incandescent light bulb, Edison had to try *six hundred* different materials before he found the right one to serve as the filament. Ask yourself: after how many attempts would you have given up? Ten? Twenty? Fifty? Would you honestly have kept going after even a hundred unsuccessful tries? We consider Edison a genius, and so he was. But would we have known of his genius if he had stopped after his five-hundredth experiment? How much perseverance was needed to give Edison's genius a chance to shine!

Henry Drummond tells the story of a man in the last century who spent a year and a half of his life, and more than $150,000, mining for gold. He was *certain* there was gold in a particular mountain, and he set out to find it. He drilled a mine a mile deep without success. Finally, frustrated and dejected, he quit and sold the mine for next to nothing. Can you guess what happened? The next man dug one yard farther and struck gold!

OVERCOMING SETBACKS

Second, *we must not be deterred by major setbacks along the way.* Financial reverses. Health problems. Natural disasters. Many people, when they encounter such difficulties and see their progress diminished, simply give up.

William Carey, the father of the modern missionary movement, left London in 1795 to begin a mission to India. During the first seven years he did not see a single person convert to Christ. Not one! But Carey pressed on. He studied the local languages and dialects, developed dictionaries and lexicons, and began the painstaking task of translating the Bible into the strange native tongues.

One day the missionary returned from a journey and found that his house had burned to the ground. The fire had destroyed several translations of the Bible and, even worse, the dictionaries and lexicons from which they had been made. What did Carey do? He got down on his knees and thanked God for the privilege of serving him. Then he simply started over. He reproduced all the work he had done, and then went on from there. How many of us could have persevered through such a disaster?

After those seven years of fruitlessness, when he had seen not a single soul come to Christ, William Carey received a letter asking him how his prospects looked. He replied that his prospects were as bright as the promises of God!

"EVERYONE LAUGHED"

Third, *we must not be deterred by the riaicule of others.* I think of a young man who believed God had called him to preach. One Sunday he stood in the pulpit to deliver his very first sermon. He had learned his message thoroughly and committed it to memory. He had practiced it over and over, honing it to perfection. The young preacher read his Scripture passage, closed his Bible, looked out over the congregation, and . . . nothing! He had forgotten his message completely. He stood there in silence for what seemed like the longest two minutes in all eternity. Then, with red face and trembling hands, he sat down in utter humiliation. Did this man give up? Did he conclude from his shame that he had been wrong about God's call on his life? No. He came back and tried again. His name was David Livingstone, the world's best-known missionary to Africa.

I think of another man, giving his very first speech in the British Parliament. His oratorical skill was so limited, he expressed himself so poorly, he stumbled over his words so badly, that his listeners began to guffaw. Before he finished, virtually the entire House of Commons was in an uproar. Finally he sat down and covered his face with his hands, in utter shame and disgrace. But someone heard him say, "You may laugh at me now, but the time will come when you shall listen to what I have to say." Every history student knows that Benjamin Disraeli went on to be a brilliant orator, and one of Britain's greatest prime ministers.

I cannot count the number of letters I have received over the years from people who have fallen into discouragement because they tried something and "everyone laughed." It may have been complete strangers who ridiculed them. Or it may have been someone quite close to them—a friend, a parent, a spouse. But my answer is always the same: never give up. Don't quit because others laugh. Persevere, and the last laugh may be yours!

THE ATTITUDE OF INGRATITUDE

Finally, *we must not be deterred by the ingratitude of those we try to help.* I suppose nothing is more disheartening than to pour out our time and energy for another person, only to have our efforts ignored—or, even worse, denigrated. How well do parents know the feeling! So do doctors, nurses, pastors, social workers—anyone who has ever tried to help others.

What are we to do? If the ingratitude of others has turned us from our task, we need to remind ourselves that we are really working for another, for the one whose voice will someday say to us, "Well done, thou good and faithful servant" (Matthew 25:21).

STRENGTH TO PERSEVERE

Where do we find the strength to persevere? The Bible tells us:

... They that wait upon the LORD shall renew their strength; they shall mount up with wings as eagles; they shall run, and not be weary; and they shall walk and not faint. Isaiah 40:31

Here, then, is the secret. We must stay close to God and seek him in prayer and in his Word, the Bible. We must remember his promise that "in due season we *shall* reap, if we faint not." The farmer knows where this metaphor comes from. He knows what it means to work in harmony with the unseen forces of nature so that if he faithfully sows, and waters, and weeds, the day will come when he will most certainly reap the harvest. The promises of God are every bit as reliable. If we place our trust in them, if we wait upon the Lord, we shall indeed see the fruit.

What about you? Have you been a quitter? Have you been tempted to give up? Once you have a clear vision of what God is calling you to do—and once you are certain it is from God—determine to see it through.

F.B. Meyer was a man of tremendous talent. When he announced his intention to go into the ministry, his mother was concerned about his reduced prospects for financial reward. She finally concluded that if he did go into the ministry, and it did not work out, he could always go into something else.

"Never!" he replied. "That would be to set my hand to the plow and then turn back." Meyer went on to become a saintly man and a minister much used by God. He did indeed set his hand to the plow, and he never turned back. And God, who had called him, never abandoned him.

Have you been afraid to begin? I challenge you: begin today! Have you begun and then quit? I urge you: begin again! And this time make up your mind to stand firm on the promises of God. As an old preacher once said, "Perseverance is very simple. You simply take hold, hold on, and never let go." God grant such perseverance to you and to me!

FIFTEEN

The Christian's Magic Wand

Be careful for nothing; but in every thing by prayer and supplication with thanksgiving let your requests be made known unto God. And the peace of God, which passeth all understanding, shall keep your hearts and minds through Christ Jesus. **Philippians 4:6-7**

DO YOU REMEMBER READING fairy tales as a child about wonderful magicians with their magic wands? They would simply wave their wands and—poof!—something would be instantly and gloriously transformed. I'm sure there are very few of us who did not wish, deep in our hearts, to have a magic wand of our own. Think how many unpleasant aspects of life could have been changed into something wonderful!

Well, I believe that the Lord *has* offered something very much like a magic wand—something with which we are all familiar, but something we take very much for granted. What is it? *Thanksgiving.* Thanksgiving is, of course, the outward expression of the inward attitude of *gratitude*. It can work like a magic wand upon the circumstances of our life.

Someone has said that gratitude is the most deified, and yet the most deserted, of virtues. That is, we love to sing its praises, but we practice it only sparingly. We even need to set aside a special holiday once a year, just to remind ourselves to give thanks. But how much thought do we give to expressing our gratitude once the fourth Thursday of November has passed each year?

OVERCOMING ANXIETY

Let's talk about some of the particular ways in which thanksgiving can help turn the base metals of life into gold. The first is that *thanksgiving can transform anxiety into peace.*

Like all pastors' wives, my wife Anne has to cope with a fair amount of pressure that comes from living with a minister. One day, she remembers, was particularly stressful, her schedule even more packed than usual. She was under pressure to get a great many things done, and she did not see how she was going to accomplish them all. To make matters worse, every time she got started on some project, she would be interrupted by a telephone call. (I don't know if you are aware of this, but telephones in parsonages seem to ring approximately every seventeen seconds.) Anne was starting to get quite anxious about how she was going to get everything done.

Then my wife remembered that on top of everything

else, she needed to call her prayer partners from our church's evangelism program. She decided, for no particular reason, to do that first. That was one of the best decisions she ever made. Anne called each of them in turn, listened to them tell about how the Lord had been blessing their efforts to tell others about himself. She prayed for their various needs and thanked God for his love and mercy and faithfulness. By the time she had finished, all her anxiety was gone, and her heart was filled with peace.

"Well," my wife thought to herself, "what else should I have expected? The Bible says to make our requests known to God 'by prayer and supplication with thanksgiving,' and then 'the peace that passes all understanding' will rule in our hearts. That's what I did, and that's just what happened."

No doubt you remember the words of the old hymn:

Count your many blessings,
  Name them one by one;
And it will surprise you
  What the Lord has done.

It really works, you know. By the time you get through naming all your blessings—counting them one by one, being surprised again at all God has done for you—you will conclude that it really does not make sense to be anxious when you know a God who has cared for you in so many ways. Surely he will not forsake you now!

Whenever you are experiencing anxiety, use the magic wand of thanksgiving to turn it to peace.

EVERYDAY MIRACLES

Second, *thanksgiving can transform the commonplace into the sacred.* William Paley, a great apologist for Christianity, once said that the main reason for our insensibility to the goodness of our creator is the very vastness of his bounty. God is *so* good to us, so overwhelmingly gracious, that we take his goodness for granted. We simply pass over the commonplace, everyday occurrences of life without recognizing God's hand in them, without acknowledging his role or giving thanks to him.

Yet if these very same events happened but once in our lifetime, they would be considered miraculous. Suppose there had never been a baby born into the world. No one had ever seen a baby. People just arrived on the scene fully grown in some way. And then, one day, a woman had a baby. What a wonder! That birth would be recorded on the front page of every newspaper in the world! It would be considered a miracle! Well, the fact that hundreds of thousands of babies are born into the world each day does not make each and every one of them any less a miracle.

Or suppose there had never been such a thing as wheat. Then, one day, someone discovered it, and they set before you a hot, delicious slice of buttered bread. Never before had such a thing existed! What a miracle! Well, you and I know that there are millions of loaves of bread baked every day. But the Christian can see that God has a hand in every one of them. Behind the bread is the baker; behind the baker is the miller; behind the miller is the farmer; behind the farmer are the wind and rain and sun; and behind the wind and rain and sun is the hand of God.

Thanksgiving looks beyond all the intermediaries and sees the ultimate source: the loving providence of God. It transforms the commonplace into the sacred. As we begin to give thanks to God, we become aware of his presence. We find ourselves in an enchanted land, a land divine, a land full with the presence of the great creator. Our spiritual eyes are opened, and everything is changed. The ordinary dons a halo. A meal becomes a sacrament. Daily work becomes a divine privilege. Conversation becomes *koinonia*: heavenly fellowship. A night's rest becomes a nestling among the angels. The magic wand of thanksgiving works all these transformations, and more!

WARDING OFF SIN

Third, *thanksgiving can transform temptation into triumph*. In the first chapter of his letter to the Romans, Paul catalogs the tremendous list of sins into which the pagan world falls. It is interesting that near the top of the list are these words: "Neither were thankful" (Romans 1:21). The precipitous slide into sin involves ingratitude.

That shouldn't surprise us, should it? It works in just the same way for us as individuals. You are not going to commit adultery if you are truly thankful for your husband or wife. You are not going to steal something if you are grateful for what you have. You are not going to envy the talents or abilities of someone else if you are grateful for those that God has given you. You are not going to grumble and complain about your life if you are thankful for where God has situated you.

Nor can you be proud if you are genuinely thankful to God. Pride is simply a matter of gratitude stopping with self. It is giving thanks to ourselves for what we have and who we are, rather than giving thanks to God.

Whenever you are tempted to sin, consider the ways in which that temptation might stem from ingratitude. Then set about giving thanks to God for whatever seems relevant. Wave the magic wand of thanksgiving, and you will see that temptation begin to lose its power.

GRATEFUL FOR ONE ANOTHER

Fourth, *thanksgiving can transform a despondent person into a cheerful person.* I know a woman who was going through her first Thanksgiving holiday without her recently deceased husband. She was desolate. She felt that life had no meaning for her. Then someone happened to say to her, "You know, I'm so thankful to God for you." That simple statement opened a well of gratitude in her heart. "All is not over!" she thought. "Someone still appreciates me. I'm still good for something. Life *is* worth living!"

In Africa a group of Ugandan Christians have a custom. Whenever they pass another Christian at work or in the market, they say, "Thank you, brother," or, "Thank you, sister." They thereby acknowledge their interdependence, that each one depends in some way upon the others. We all need to thank one another—simply for being there.

When was the last time you told someone, "I'm thankful to God for you"? Those words could mean so much. Life becomes burdensome to everyone at one time or another.

All of us can use the lift that gratitude brings.

This is true even of people who seem to "have it made." I have had the opportunity of meeting many successful men and women in my life, including the heads of many Christian organizations. One thing I have found to be true of all of them is that they are carrying tremendous burdens, and often are struggling simply to keep their heads above water. One man I know said he often felt as though he were in the middle of the ocean—with five ropes in his mouth tied to five boats he was trying to tow to shore—about to go under for the third time.

The tragedy is that the average person usually supposes such leaders to be sitting serenely atop the mountain of success. Some even seem to think that their calling in life is to throw stones at such people, to keep them from becoming too proud or secure. Seldom do people realize that even those whose circumstances seem enviable are in need of the encouragement that a simple expression of gratitude can bring.

BONDS OF FRIENDSHIP

Finally, *thanksgiving can transform mere acquaintances into friends.* There are few things that bind people together more firmly than a recognition of how grateful they are for one another. Conversely, there are few things that drive people apart more effectively than ingratitude. Thanklessness is treason against our fellow man.

Yet most of us have received innumerable benefits from other people for which we have never expressed thankfulness. Do you doubt it? Just think of some people who are close to you, and imagine how your life would be different if they had never lived. It is tragic how many times our expressions of gratitude for others are held back until they have passed away. We are accustomed to hearing eulogies only at funerals. How much better if people could hear how thankful others are for them while they are still alive!

If you would bind people to your heart with bands of iron—and here I emphatically include wives and husbands, parents and children—let them know often how grateful you are that God has brought them into your life.

WHAT SIZE IS YOUR SOUL?

Lack of gratitude, according to the Scripture, is a tragic fault. Every parent knows how hurtful it can be to have an ungrateful child. For us to be ungrateful toward God is just as hurtful to him.

One author described a fictional character named Edith as "a small country, bounded on the north, the south, the east, and the west by Edith." I can tell you one thing about Edith, and that is that she was an ungrateful person. The rivers that flowed into Edith, as far as she could tell, flowed only from the northern land of Edith. In her mind, there was nothing for which to be grateful.

Small-souled persons are niggardly with their gratitude. They are more likely to express ingratitude, even criticism. Usually this is because they have not learned their true value in God's eyes. Because they are small in their own estimation, they try to cut everyone else down to the same size. The only way they know how to build themselves up is to tear others down.

Large-souled persons, on the other hand, exude thankfulness. They recognize what others have done and are doing for them, and express gratitude to them. More important, they recognize what God has done and is doing for them, and give thanks to him.

Let me encourage you to become a large-souled person by becoming more thankful. Give thanks to God daily for his love and mercy toward you. Count your many blessings; number them one by one. Express gratitude to the countless people through whom God has chosen to pour out his blessings upon you. You will be amazed at how the magic wand of thanksgiving can transform your life!

SIXTEEN

How to Be Happy

Rejoice in the Lord alway: and again I say, Rejoice.

Philippians 4:4

W HAT WOULD YOU REALLY LIKE TO GET out of life? What are you honestly seeking?

Most people, if they answered that question honestly, would probably say they are just trying to get through life with a little happiness, just seeking a bit of joy in their earthly existence.

That desire, of course, is the essence of hedonism, a philosophy of life that sees no farther than the gratification of our appetite for pleasure. Even so, most errors contain at least a grain of truth, and such is the case even with hedonism.

ENJOY GOD?

Is there anything wrong with being happy, from the Christian point of view? To look at many congregations on an average Sunday, you might think there was! Many church folks seem to treat happiness as impious at best and ungodly at worst, and to think that proper worship requires a long face and a turned-down mouth.

But that is not the way it needs to be. The first question in the Westminster Shorter Catechism asks, "What is the chief end of man?" The answer: "The chief end of man is to glorify God and to enjoy him forever." Do you *enjoy* God? Have you ever even thought in terms of enjoying him?

Most people look upon religion as something to be tolerated, certainly not as something to be enjoyed. Yet down through the centuries, the greatest saints have been people who have somehow discovered tremendous joy in their faith. They have seen the nuggets of gold deeply embedded in the trying circumstances of life.

What about you? Have you discovered joy in your walk with God? You can!

SATAN'S GREATEST LIE

First we need to expose what is probably Satan's greatest lie. For centuries he has been telling it to men and women in all walks of life. Though it may be expressed in different ways, in essence Satan says, "God wants you to be miserable, but I want you to be happy."

Satan's basic propaganda goes back to the beginning. Remember what he said to Eve? "Did God tell you not to eat the fruit of that tree? Why, God knows that if you eat it, you will become like him! He's jealous! He's trying to hold you down. If you eat the fruit of that tree, your life will be expanded, enriched. You'll know happiness beyond anything you've ever imagined."

Eve bought Satan's lie. She ate. And she died.

Satan has been telling us the same lie ever since. He says it to you and me even today: "God wants you to have all the things that look bad, taste bitter, and make you appear stupid in the eyes of others. The whole world is going to laugh at you if you get caught up in this religion thing. I offer you things that look good and taste sweet and make others look at you with envy."

Have you ever heard that pitch? I suppose all of us have fallen for it at one time or another. "God wants us sad, Satan wants us glad." That is the lie. What a colossal deception!

REJOICE

Against all this, we are confronted by the startling exhortation of Scripture, "Rejoice in the Lord always!" Isn't that amazing? God is telling us to rejoice! It is virtually in the form of a commandment.

That may seem a bit odd to us. How can we be commanded to rejoice? Isn't joy something that "just happens" inside us as a result of good things happening *to* us? Isn't joy therefore something outside of our control?

Yes and no. There is an emotion of joy that does "just happen" to us when things go our way. But rejoicing can also be a deliberately chosen *action* on our part. The Greek word is *chairoie*, which speaks of purposeful, deliberate activity: to be glad, to sing aloud, to leap with joy. We can—and the Bible says we should—decide to rejoice. When was the last time you leaped for joy? Yet that is what God calls us to do.

THE TESTIMONY OF JOY

Why does God give us this exhortation or command-ment to rejoice? First of all, I think it is because *rejoicing is a tremendous testimony* to God's goodness, to his faithfulness, to his love. It testifies to the truthfulness of his Word. Sadness in a Christian can appear to be a testimony to all the opposite traits.

Rejoicing is such a marvelous testimony because it "baits the hook" with the one thing people want most in this world—to be happy. Human beings spend most of their waking hours seeking something to fill the emptiness in their souls. They are seeking joy. If you can offer them that, people will be eager to learn your secret.

F.B. Meyer, the great preacher of yesteryear, said he was brought to Christ by observing the exuberant joy in the face of a young man who had recently committed his life to God. The man's joy was irresistible, he said. Just to see it was to hunger for it. So he sought it, he found it, and he, too, went on his way rejoicing.

What a wonderful testimony to Christ is joy! Jesus himself said joy was like a spring of water that wells up in the soul and overflows to others. It is a river that sparkles in the sunshine of God's grace. Joy shines forth from the eye and resonates in the voice, drawing people irresistibly to its source, which is Christ. No wonder God, who wants all men and women to come to know his Son, wants us to rejoice!

A STRENGTH AND SHIELD

Another reason God calls us to "rejoice always" is that *rejoicing gives us strength.*

Have you ever had "one of those days?" You've been working hard all day—at the office, at school, around the house—and are just worn out. Dog tired. Exhausted. You have no energy even to think about doing anything.

Then the phone rings. It's an old friend, someone you haven't heard from in years. Your friend is in town unexpectedly and wants to see you—tonight! What happens? All of a sudden the tiredness seems to melt away. Enthusiasm floods your heart and invigorates your body. Why? Joy at the prospect of seeing your old friend again has brought you to life!

Joy gives strength for living. It gives wings to our feet. Our steps are lightened when our hearts are filled with joy. The best part is that the same benefits result whether joy "just happens" to us, or whether it flows from our *decision* to rejoice in the goodness of our God. The joy of the Lord truly is our strength! (See Nehemiah 8:10.)

A third reason God urges us to "rejoice always" is because *rejoicing protects us from temptation.* Have you ever noticed how much easier it is to fall into sin when you are "down in the dumps?" When we are unhappy, we look for something to fill the inner void—and sometimes we look in the wrong places. But when we are rejoicing, we have less room in our hearts for sin. The voice of the tempter meets greater resistence.

THE DOUBLE ANTIDOTE

Paul's exhortation to "rejoice always" is surrounded on either side by two very interesting texts. On the one side is Paul's discussion about two women in the church at Philippi who are "having it out." Paul urges them to be of one mind. On the other side is Paul's admonition about anxiety: "Be careful for nothing" (Philippians 4:6). Rejoicing is like a mountain peak, rising up between the valleys of interpersonal problems and worry.

Joy is, indeed, an antidote to both. Perhaps you have not noticed, but happy people have very few enemies. The person who has trouble getting along with others is often the one who is morose, down in the mouth, unhappy. People do not respond well to someone like that. The joyful person, on the other hand, is easy for others to relate to. He is not quick to take offense, nor does he often give offense. Rather, he brings gladness into every situation.

A joyful husband brings happiness into his home. A wife who rejoices will not have the troubles that an unhappy wife will encounter. What a wonderful thing to walk into a home and hear singing, or better yet, bring singing with you. How often does either happen in your home? Scripture calls us to rejoice, to leap with joy, to break forth with singing.

As to anxiety: joy simply drives it away. True joy, the joy that comes from the Holy Spirit, brings with it God's power to chase worries away.

THE SOURCE OF JOY

What is the source of true joy? Where does it come from? When God calls us to rejoice, does he mean we are to go around *pretending* to be happy, putting on a false face? Of course not. But where is joy to be found?

The Scripture says, "In thy presence is fulness of joy; at thy right hand there are pleasures for evermore" (Psalm 16:11). There is the secret! The answer is simple: the fullness of joy is found in the presence of God. As we spend time with the Lord, his joy is infused into our souls. We discover, in contradiction to Satan's great lie, that Christ is no cosmic killjoy. Rather, he is the source of all happiness.

"Ah," you say, "but doesn't the Bible describe Jesus as "a man of sorrows, and acquainted with grief" (Isaiah 53:3)? Indeed it does. And indeed he was. Jesus was acquainted with *our* grief. He bore *our* sorrows, *our* sins. He received *our* chastisement and *our* punishment, so that *we* might be able to rejoice.

Jesus is the source of joy—a joy that does not depend upon outward circumstances. Human happiness, which is much more shallow, depends upon happenings to bring happiness. But Jesus brings a joy that is untouched by the circumstances of life. It was, after all, awaiting execution from inside a Roman dungeon, that Paul said, "Rejoice!" Clearly he knew a joy that did not depend merely on his "having a nice day!"

Jesus is the source of joy. Our joy is, in fact, a barometer of our closeness to him. Our silence in song indicates the poverty of our prayer. If we do not leap with joy, it is because we do not often enough bend the knee. If we are empty inside, it is because we have not allowed Jesus to fill us with the love, peace, and joy of his Spirit.

THE GREAT HINDRANCE

The great hindrance to joy is, of course, sin. Sin is like a film that coats the soul and robs it of its sparkle. Sin makes us like a crystal chandelier that has hung too long without being cleaned, until it has lost its lustre. But if it is cleaned and the film washed away, the chandelier of our soul will once again shine forth with all the colors of the rainbow.

So it is with us and joy. When we are forgiven, the film of sin is washed away and our joy can shine forth. When God gets rid of the last vestige of sin in our lives, we will be in heaven, where there is eternal joy. "In thy presence is joy forevermore."

Lovelessness, which is the ultimate sin, will rob us of joy more quickly and more ruthlessly than anything I know. Are you holding animosity toward someone else? If so, you are depriving yourself of the most glorious experience you can know in this life: the richness of the joy of the Lord, which is the aura of the heart where his love resides.

REJOICE *ALWAYS*

When are we to rejoice? Incredibly, Paul says we are to rejoice *always*. At all times. All day. Every day.

But there are so many times when we do not feel like rejoicing, when things are going badly, when the whole world seems to be against us. We simply do not feel happy. But remember: happiness depends on happenings, but joy comes from Jesus.

Whatever else may be happening in our lives, we can rejoice in God and his salvation. We can rejoice in his mercy and forgiveness. We can rejoice in the hope of eternal life. We can rejoice in the providence that watches over our lives, working all things together for good.

"Rejoice always." That includes *right now*. Are you rejoicing in the Lord? If not, why not? There is no substitute for that time in Christ's presence when we can be filled with his joy. We cannot fake joy. We cannot "work it up." We can only *receive* it from the Spirit of God.

Henry Van Dyke, the great poet, wrote:

Joy is a duty: so with golden lore
    The rabbis taught in days of yore
And human hearts heard in their speech
    The lightest wisdom man can reach.
But one bright peak rises far above
    Where the Master stands, whose name is Love
Saying to those whom heavy tasks employ
    Life is divine when duty is a joy.

And, we might add, life is divine when joy is a duty to which we apply ourselves by God's grace: "Rejoice evermore. Pray without ceasing. In every thing give thanks: for this is the will of God in Christ Jesus concerning you" (1 Thessalonians 5:16-18).

SEVENTEEN

Surmounting the Insurmountable

And it shall come to pass, as soon as the soles of the feet of the priests that bear the ark of the LORD, the Lord of all the earth, shall rest in the waters of Jordan, that the waters of Jordan shall be cut off from the waters that come down from above; and they shall stand upon an heap. Joshua 3:13

ALL OF US HAVE SEEN the famous painting of Washington crossing the Delaware. He did it at a time when it was thought to be impossible, thus taking the British by surprise. Many centuries before, Xerxes crossed the Hellespont with two million men, and took the Greeks by surprise.

I would like to tell you of a crossing far more marvelous than either of these. Washington used boats, and Xerxes used an improvised bridge. But the Word of God tells us of a time when thousands of Israelites crossed the Jordan River, at the height of its annual flood tide, *on dry land.* This amazing incident has taken the entire world by surprise for more than three thousand years! And it is filled with lessons for us today.

WANDERING THE WILDERNESS

Let me remind you of the setting in which this remarkable event took place. Through ten horrible plagues, God had acted to deliver his people from their cruel taskmasters in Egypt. By his outstretched arm, he had brought them out of Egypt through the Red Sea.

The Israelites had then sent twelve spies into the land of Canaan, to reconnoiter the land God had promised to deliver into their hands. They returned saying it was indeed a marvelous land, flowing with milk and honey. *But,* they said, it was also a terrifying land, populated by giants before whom the Israelites would look like grasshoppers. Confronting these fearsome opponents seemed unthinkable.

At least, it seemed unthinkable to *some* of the spies. Joshua and Caleb, as we have already seen, brought the minority report. "Yes," they said, "the cities are walled. Yes, the men are giants. But there is nothing too hard for our God to handle. Let us rise up and go forward."

But the people refused to be encouraged. They murmured. They grumbled. They complained. And, in the end, they refused to go. "Why have you brought us out into the desert to die?" they whined to Moses. "Weren't there enough graves in Egypt?"

God was angry with the Israelites for their hardness of heart—so much so that he declared that not a single one of them would see the fulfillment of his promise. The Lord condemned them to wander back and forth, up and down, across the wilderness for forty years—long enough for every adult member of that rebellious generation to die.

FLOOD TIDE

At last their years of wandering came to an end. The Israelites found themselves at the shore of the Jordan River at full flood tide, its waters roaring down from the Sea of Galilee into the Dead Sea. From where they stood, the Israelites could see the promised land, the long-awaited fulfillment of their dreams. So many years, so many hardships, so many disappointments—and now there it was, beckoning to them.

Only one obstacle remained in their way: the Jordan. At flood tide it was several hundred feet wide, and perhaps thirty feet deep. No doubt a strong man could swim it. But thousands of men, women, and children, with all their herds and flocks, their tents and other possessions, to say nothing of the tabernacle of the Lord—there was no way that such a multitude could possibly ford the river. And just beyond the Jordan River stood the fortified city of Jericho, whose hostile inhabitants stood watching from the city walls. God's people appeared to be facing a truly insurmountable obstacle.

THE TERROR OF THE NEW

At their head stood Joshua, the man God had selected to succeed Moses as captain of Israel's army. It was Joshua, one of the two faithful spies, who was to lead God's people into the land of promise.

Interestingly, the name "Joshua" is really the same as the name "Jesus." Jesus is the Greek version of the Hebrew name *Yeshua,* which our English translations of the Old Testament usually render "Joshua." Jesus, in other words, is our Joshua, the captain of the host of the Lord who leads us from bondage into freedom.

God tells Joshua to prepare the people to cross the river, and he notes that "Ye have not passed this way heretofore" (Joshua 3:4). They had wandered the desert to the north, south, east, and west, but now they faced a totally unprecedented situation. Here was something new: a new danger, a new obstacle, a new fear to be confronted.

Do we not all face similar situations at times? Into the midst of our familiar routine bursts something new, something unexpected. We fear the unknown. We have enough trouble facing "the same old problems." Facing new difficulties is even more unsettling. God wants to reassure us, even as he reassured the Israelites, that though our situation may be unprecedented in *our* experience, it is not beyond *his* ability to handle. It is as though he were saying, "I know you have not passed this way before. I know you are frightened. But don't be. Place your trust in me."

"SANCTIFY YOURSELVES"

Next, notice an interesting direction that God gives Joshua for the people. "Sanctify yourselves," he says, "for tomorrow the Lord will do wonders among you" (Joshua 3:5).

What a magnificent promise! "God will do great things in your midst, among you and through you and by you." I suspect all of us desire that God would do wonders in our midst, to use us to do great things for the sake of the gospel.

If that is to happen, one thing is needful: *sanctify yourselves.* The great physician does not operate with a dirty scalpel. "Who shall ascend into the hill of the LORD?" asks the psalmist. The answer: "He that hath clean hands, and a pure heart" (see Psalm 24:3, 4). Therefore sanctify your-selves: cleanse your hands and your hearts.

Are you wholly sold out to Jesus Christ? "Give me twelve men completely dedicated to Christ," Dwight Moody once said, "and I will change this city." Would you be one of those twelve? You who would walk with one foot in the kingdom of this world and one in the kingdom of God, you who would place your trust in the things of this world as well as in the things of God, be single-minded. Yield yourselves completely to God. Confess your sins. Ask God to fill you with his Spirit, to make you wholly his in body, mind, and soul, so that in every way you might belong to him.

THE LIVING GOD

"Hereby ye shall know that the living God is among you," Joshua said, "and that he will without fail drive out from before you the Canaanites" (Joshua 3:10). It is the *living* God who was among them, not some lifeless idol like the "gods" worshiped by the Canaanites, the Hittites, the Hivites, and all the others.

If you give yourself over to be a soldier of Jesus Christ—if you are determined to occupy the land on his behalf, to drive out the heathen by transforming them into living believers in Christ—then you shall indeed know that the living God is among you. He *makes* himself known to those who cast their lot with him.

One of the reasons why so many have weak faith and little hope is because they have not made up their minds to be used by God. They have never so much as lifted a sword against the modern-day Canaanites that surround them. They have never seen anyone quake before the power of the gospel, because they have never dared open their mouths to speak it. If they would, God would rush to their side and make himself known in their midst!

THE FOOT OF FAITH

It was *as the feet of the priests touched the water* that the mighty Jordan would begin to recede. Not before then. God would make his power manifest *as they took action in obedience to him.*

When the Israelites stood fifty feet from the banks of the river, the Jordan was still formidable. When they were twenty feet away, it was just as formidable. When they were but five feet away, it seemed even more insurmountable an obstacle than it had from a mile away. When they were only one foot away, there still was not the slightest indication that help was coming.

Yet the instant the feet of the priests touched the waters, the flow was cut off. It was as though God had taken a great sheet of glass and planted it amidst the mighty river. The waters piled up in a crystal wall.

So it is with many of the obstacles we face. They flee at the first touch of faith. We sometimes speak of "the hand of faith"—reaching out to take hold of Jesus Christ. We might just as well speak of "the foot of faith," stepping forward in faith-filled obedience to God's commands. The Bible describes life as a journey, a pilgrimage. Many times we must, in faith, step forward into a seemingly insurmountable obstacle. It will be *as we do so* that God will make himself real to us.

What would have happened if the Israelites had simply sat down in their tents and observed the Jordan from a safe distance? "Well, if God would simply provide a way across, naturally we would be glad to go forward. As soon as we see the path appear, we'll make haste to set out." Had they done so, their bones would be resting on the near side of the river today. The river did not recede, the path did not become clear, until the foot of faith touched the waters.

NEVER HALFWAY

Notice that when God acts on our behalf, he acts with thoroughness, with perfection. He did not require the Israelites to wade through three or four feet of water. He did not even stop the waters and allow them to slog knee-deep through the mud and slime that must have lined the river bed. The Bible says that they went across "on dry ground." How astonishing that God would do such a thing! How thorough, how complete, how perfect was the miracle he performed!

Many times in my own life I have faced problems I did not have the slightest idea how to solve. They seemed destined to overwhelm me like the flood tide of the Jordan. But astonishingly, as I stepped forward, the foot of faith seemed to cut off the waters and I was able to pass through the difficulty dry-shod. When God does something, he never does it halfway.

THE FINAL OBSTACLE

The river Jordan has long been used as a symbol for the final obstacle we all face, the humanly insurmountable obstacle of death:

> On Jordan's stormy banks I stand
>   And cast a wishful eye
> To Canaan's fair and happy land,
>   Where my possessions lie.

The river of death is one that we must all cross one day; a river which for many seems exceedingly hopeless; a river that seems to gurgle forth from depths of darkness; a river upon whose surface swirl fearful mists; a river where the air is filled with moaning and groaning.

We draw back in horror from the river of death, this dark stream into which each person must plunge. But we must remember that when the priests who carried the ark of God stepped into the Jordan and saw the waters flee, it was but a foreshadowing of the day when Jesus, the great high priest of God, would come to the river of death.

God did not ordain that the waters should flee at the first touch of Jesus' foot. Rather, we know that the waters rose above his feet and ankles, to his knees, to his waist, to his chest, to his neck, until finally with the cry, "It is finished!" Jesus sank beneath death's dark billows. All the waves of God's wrath swept over him as he paid the penalty for sin that we rightly deserved. The tables of the law—which were contained within the ark on the shoulders of the priests who crossed Jordan—had now unleashed their full fury upon the great high priest as he hung upon the cross.

But when all seemed dark, when it seemed all hope had been lost, when it seemed life itself had been swallowed up by death—suddenly we saw Jesus emerge on the other side and step onto Canaan's soil. "I am he that liveth and was dead," he cries. "Behold, I am alive forevermore. He that believeth in me shall never die!"

DEATH IS SWALLOWED UP IN VICTORY

We who trust in Jesus Christ, who bear within our hearts the ark of the Lord, with its mercy seat, and the cross of Christ, and the law of God inscribed on the tablets of our soul—we can know that when our foot touches the brim of that fearful Jordan, the waters shall flee away:

O death, where is thy sting? O grave, where is thy victory? The sting of death is sin; and the strength of sin is the law. But thanks be to God, which giveth us the victory through our Lord Jesus Christ. 1 Corinthians 15:55-57

If we trust in Christ, then that awesome, dark, and deadly river loses its sting and its terror. We may fix our eyes upon Canaan's fair and happy land, knowing that there our great high priest has gone to prepare us a place.

We do not plunge beneath the river. We are not drowned in it or destroyed by it. We cross over to the other side! Amidst the trumpets and the hallelujahs of the saints, we are received by the angels of paradise into that mansion which Christ has gone ahead to prepare.

What a hope, what a confidence, what an assurance, is ours! For we know that the divine alchemist will, at the end, work the greatest transformation of all, transforming even the base metal of death and decay into the gold of everlasting life:

> ... We shall not all sleep, but we shall all be changed, in a moment, in the twinkling of an eye, at the last trump: for the trumpet shall sound, and the dead shall be raised incorruptible, and we shall be changed. For this corruptible must put on incorruption, and this mortal must put on immortality.
>
> So when this corruptible shall have put on incorruption, and this mortal shall have put on immortality, then shall be brought to pass the saying that is written, Death is swallowed up in victory. 1 Corinthians 15:51-54

EIGHTEEN

Possibilities Unlimited!

I can do all things through Christ which strengtheneth me.

Philippians 4:13

"THE ONLY THEME IN HISTORY worth mentioning," H.G. Wells once said, "the theme beside which all other themes pale into insignificance, is the theme of faith versus unbelief." Nothing, I think, could be more true.

The great tests of life are, at their core, tests of faith. Do you believe? Do you trust the living God? Is your life based upon his promises?

I am convinced that in the final analysis, all of life—both in this world and in the world to come—will come down to the promises of God. Everything good that happens to us is but the outworking of God's promises, and of our claiming those promises. When the scroll is unrolled in heaven, we will find that countless blessings we knew in this life came to us for one reason: because we believed and accepted and acted upon the promises of God.

At the same time, I believe we will discover that there were innumerable blessings we *could* have received but did not, simply because we did not know of them—or, if we did, failed to claim them and enable God to fulfill them in our lives. God's promises are like checks, drawn on the bank of heaven and signed by the Almighty. But many are never presented for payment. They lay on the shelf, in a closed Bible, unclaimed, uncashed.

GOD'S LIGHTNING

One such promise is Philippians 4:13: "I can do all things through Christ which strengtheneth me." Possibilities unlimited! If Christians would believe and act on this promise, we could transform the world.

Do you believe what this verse says? Be careful! Don't just nod your head and say, "Why, yes, of course I do." I am fairly sure that the vast majority of us do *not* really believe it. We *say* we do. In a certain intellectual way, we acknowledge that since it is in the Bible, it must be the truth.

But if we really believed this promise, to the point that we were willing to *act* on it, our lives would demonstrate it. We would expect great things from God. We would attempt great things for God. And we would see them happen!

Why is it that some Christians accomplish more in one lifetime than huge congregations of church-goers combined? Because they believe this promise! They are men and women who have taken hold of this verse by faith. They have seen the lightning of God's omnipotence flash from heaven and energize their lives. They have allowed the great alchemist to take the base metals of their hurts, pains, discouragements, fears, worries, and hardships— and turn them to gold!

Where today are those who will turn the world upside down? Where are the Deborahs? The Pauls? The Hudson Taylors? The Adoniram Judsons? The William Careys? Many men and women who believed God could do mighty things through them have seen those mighty things come to pass. Where are the men and women of today who will follow their example?

ACTING ON GOD'S PROMISES

There is really nothing all that strange or mysterious about trusting in, and acting upon, the promises of God. Is it not true that each of us became a Christian by believing God's promise? "Believe on the Lord Jesus Christ, and thou shalt be saved," Scripture says (Acts 16:31). And faith responds, "Yes, Lord. I believe in you. I believe your promise is true. I claim it for my own." And in just that way, we are saved! Our lives are changed. We become heirs of God. The passport to paradise comes into our possession— all because we believe the promise of God.

The same thing holds true with the promise we are now considering. "I can do all things through Christ which strengtheneth me." Are you claiming that promise as an integral part of your life? Has it been worked into the warp and woof of your soul?

You will know the answer to these questions by whether or not you are *acting* upon God's promise. How pathetic would a man be who, though he knew he had a million dollars in the bank, still went hungry day after day, sleeping in the cold with nothing but rags to keep the chill from his bones. If we believe we have this promise from God, we will act upon it, expecting God to fulfill it just as surely as he fulfills any other part of his Word. Let us not find ourselves with "just enough faith to get to heaven," but not enough to live the life of heaven here on earth!

"I CAN ..."

The verse says, "*I* can do all things through Christ," with the accent on the "I." To turn it around, this means you! *You* can do all things through Christ who strengthens you. *You.* Not someone else. Not your minister. Not some foreign missionary. Not even your spouse. *You!* You, young lady. You, young man. You with the silver hair, you whose step has been slowed by the passing of years, you who are weighed down with the cares of making a living and providing for your family. God says that *you* can do all things through Christ who strengthens you.

The verse says, "I *can* do all things through Christ." Zig Ziglar tells of an international expedition organized some years ago to climb the north wall of the Matterhorn. When reporters interviewed them, they spoke in various ways about the challenge before them. One said, "I'm going to try." Another said, "I'm going to give it my best effort." Still another said, "I'll give it everything I've got." Only one man responded, simply but firmly, "I *will* climb the north wall of the Matterhorn." When the expedition was over, only one of those men had succeeded. Care to guess which one?

"DO ALL THINGS . . ."

The verse says, "I can do *all* things." Most of us, I think, read this verse as though it said, "I can do *some* things," or "I can do a few things," or, "I can do one or two puny, insignificant things." But that is not what it says. Scripture says, "I can do *all* things."

What is it that you wish to accomplish? I know a young man who has before him a mental picture of the gleaming automobile he desires to own. He thinks about it all the time. The car is his passion, his goal. Is there anything wrong with having a goal like that? Is it biblical?

Well, Scripture does tell us to ask God for the desires of our heart. It does tell us that we are to believe that we have the promises of God—that if God has promised it, it is as good as done and we are to believe by faith that it has already come to pass.

But Scripture also tells us we are not to set our affections on things here below, but on things above. Is there anything wrong with a new car? No. But God has made us for greater things than a pile of metal. In just a few years, that young man's fancy will literally be fit for nothing but the junk heap.

God made you with an immortal soul. He fitted you for immortality. Too many people grovel in the mud flats of mere materialism. Set your affections on things above! Attempt great things for God! What if all of us focused our energies on the advancement of God's kingdom the way that young man focused his energies on a car? "They that turn many to righteousness [shall shine] as the stars for ever and ever" (see Daniel 12:3). Now, there is a goal to set your heart on!

"I can do *all* things through Christ." What vision has God given you for his cause in the world? Do you dare to believe it? To make it your magnificent obsession? To trust God to bring it to pass through you?

"THROUGH CHRIST"

Finally, the verse says, "I can do all things *through Christ.*" This last phrase is critically important. Spurgeon has said that without it, the first part of the verse would be virtual blasphemy. Jesus made it plain enough when he said, "Without me ye can do nothing" (John 15:5). But *with* him, we can do *all* things!

If our resources reach no further than our own strength, they will inevitably fail us. Consider the great Nebuchadnezzar, mighty ruler of Babylon, who once stood on the broad walls of the city with its hanging gardens and its mighty tower, boasting of the great city he had built. Not long after, God deprived him of his senses and his reason, and reduced this powerful king to the level of a brute beast.

Consider the great Persian monarch who commanded an army of a million men, facing the tiny army of the Macedonians. The king mocked his puny enemy, but was thrown back in disarray before the courage and discipline of the Macedonian phalanx under the command of Alexander the Great.

Or consider Napoleon, who set himself up like a mighty rock, against which the waves of the sea of history dashed themselves to pieces. He plucked the sun from the sky of Austria, and bade the star of Prussia to set. He watched the Kremlin go up in flames. But soon, in retreat across the Russian steppe, Napoleon saw the snow strewn with the bodies of his soldiers. He finished his days in lonely exile.

No, we need something greater than our own strength to empower our hearts and minds and souls. Only *through Christ* can we do all things.

VOICES OF GLOOM

Why do we find it so hard to accept God's Word in this marvelous promise? Because we have listened to the voices of gloom, the voices that tell us we can do nothing, that we are failures. And we have believed their lies rather than the truth of God's Word.

"You're a dunce!" the mathematics teacher said to her exasperating pupil. "You're a dunce, and I'm going to fail you!" And so she did. How do you suppose that teacher felt in later years, knowing she had given young Albert Einstein an "F" in math?

"I'm sorry," the choir director said, "but we don't want you in our choir. You can't sing. Please don't come back." But Jerome Hines went on to become one of the Metropolitan Opera's greatest basses.

"You can't do it. It's no use. Give up. Don't you remember how many times you've tried and failed?" So say the voices. Isn't it a good thing Walt Disney didn't listen? He went broke seven times before he finally succeeded. Isn't it a good thing Thomas Edison didn't listen? He had more than 14,000 failed experiments in his brilliant career. Isn't it a good thing Babe Ruth didn't listen? He had more strikeouts than any player in history—and more home runs, too.

Zig Ziglar says a big shot is just a little shot who kept on shooting. When experience told him he couldn't hit the mark, when his friends and relatives and coworkers and neighbors told him he'd never be able to shoot straight, he just cocked and aimed and kept firing.

"CALL UNTO ME"

"I can do all things through Christ which strengtheneth me." Who was it that made such a claim? It was Paul, with his thorn in the flesh and his weak eyes. Paul, the apostle who once persecuted the church of Jesus Christ, but went on to turn the whole world upside down for Christ's sake. Paul, who was willing to endure all manner of hardship in the name of his heavenly master. Five times he was scourged. Three times he was beaten with rods. Once he was stoned. Three times he was shipwrecked.

Yet, like so many others who would follow in his train, Paul attempted great things for God because he expected great things from God. He believed what God had said: "Call unto me, and I will answer thee, and show thee great and mighty things, which thou knowest not" (Jeremiah 33:3). And so Paul did precisely that!

TAPPING THE SOURCE

"I can do all things through Christ which strengtheneth me." We have available to us unlimited power for unlimited possibilities. Yet too often we do not tap into it.

It is always true that the power we see in the world around us comes from some outside source. We do not really *generate* power, we simply capture it, transform it, and then release it. A power station does not create power. It simply takes the power already resident in the river, or the coal, or the atomic fission on which it operates, and transforms that power into electricity.

It is the same with us and the power of God. We do not generate it or bring it into being. We do not "work it up." It is simply *there* for us, by the grace of God, waiting for us to tap into it. A machine in a factory may be capable of performing remarkable feats—but only if it is plugged in. A sailboat can gather the wind and hurtle across the wide sea—but only if the sail is raised. The sail that enables us to catch the wind of the Spirit of God is faith. Faith has to do with *believing* and *acting on* God's promises.

GOD'S TIMETABLE

We can do all things through Christ, but we cannot do them all at once. There is an order to God's ways. He follows a law of development. God does not simply create a giant redwood tree overnight. The mighty Sequoias of California did not arrive full grown in a single day. God arranged for them to be planted, to take root, to receive the necessary sunlight and rainwater, and to grow slowly and steadily over the centuries. It is the same with us. God's promises reach their fulfillment on his timetable, by means of his ordained process. And that process may involve its share of challenge and difficulty.

But as we hold fast to God's promises, as we set the goal before our eyes in faith, as we place our trust in the power of God to energize and work through us—even in spite of our weaknesses—we will find that by the grace of God we can move toward the goal he has given us, and can accomplish it to the glory of Jesus Christ.

What hurdles, what obstacles, can ever stand in our way when we are moving under the power of the mighty God? What problems, what difficulties, what weaknesses in our life can prevent us from accomplishing what he calls us to, so long as we rely on him? Is there any burden he will not help us to bear? Any sorrow he will not help us transcend? Any trial he will not help us endure? Any discouragement he will not help us conquer?

Of course not! Our God *will* work all things together for good to those who love him, to those who are called according to his purpose. There is no valley so deep his love cannot fill it, no mountain so high his grace cannot scale it. There is no trial, no tribulation, no fear, no anxiety, no doubt, no discouragement, no adversity, no sorrow, no grief—*nothing* whatsoever that he cannot, and *will* not, work together for our good. There is no metal so base that his love and mercy cannot turn it to gold.